# SOUL
# PRESCRIPTION

*101 Ways to Find
Joy, Meaning & Fulfillment*

# DANA LLOYD

All rights reserved.

No part of this book may be reproduced, without the author's permission, by any mechanical, digital, or photographic means. It shall not be transmitted, or otherwise be copied for public or private use. Using brief quotations for articles, social media or speeches may be used with credit given to the author. The author of this book does not provide medical advice or prescribe the use of any idea described in this book as a form of treatment for physical, emotional or medical problems without the advice of a physician, either directly or indirectly. The author's intention is to offer information of a general nature to help you in your search for emotional and spiritual growth. The ideas contained in this book are reflections of the author's personal journey. At no time, are you expected to substitute the ideas presented in this book for your own, whether stated or implied. The word *prescription* used in this book is a marketing term only, not a medical prescription. In the event, you use any of the information in this book for your personal journey or in a self-help capacity, the author assumes no responsibility for your actions.

**Soul Prescription: 101 Ways To Find Joy, Meaning & Fulfillment**
©2017 by Dana Lloyd

**ISBN**-13: 978-0995272002
**ISBN**-10: 099527200X

I. Self-Help

II. Inspiration

III. Spirituality

IV. Leadership

This book is dedicated to my mother, Rose,

my greatest spiritual teacher.

Love you, always.

## TABLE OF CONTENTS

| | | |
|---|---|---|
| Foreword | | ix |
| My Journey | | 1 |
| The Inner Critic | | 5 |
| Soul R$_x$ #1 | Relentlessly Seek Your Highest Self | 7 |

## GROWTH

| | | |
|---|---|---|
| Soul R$_x$ #2 | Growth, Not Self-Improvement | 13 |
| Soul R$_x$ #3 | Nourish Your Mind Daily | 15 |
| Soul R$_x$ #4 | Let Go | 17 |
| Soul R$_x$ #5 | Get Comfortable With Being Uncomfortable | 19 |
| Soul R$_x$ #6 | Know Your Strengths | 21 |
| Soul R$_x$ #7 | Stop It | 23 |
| Soul R$_x$ #8 | Start It | 25 |
| Soul R$_x$ #9 | Learn From Adversity | 27 |
| Soul R$_x$ #10 | Know When To Change | 29 |
| Soul R$_x$ #11 | Make Excellence Your Standard, Not Perfection | 31 |
| Soul R$_x$ #12 | Use Reflection To Grow You | 35 |
| Soul R$_x$ #13 | Allow The Big Life Questions To Transform You | 37 |

## ACCEPTANCE

| | | |
|---|---|---|
| Soul R$_x$ #14 | Be At Peace With The Pace Of Your Unfolding | 41 |
| Soul R$_x$ #15 | Honour Your Journey | 43 |
| Soul R$_x$ #16 | Accept Yourself | 45 |
| Soul R$_x$ #17 | You Are Right Where You Are Supposed To Be | 47 |

## LOVE

| | | |
|---|---|---|
| Soul R$_x$ #18 | Love Is The Way | 51 |
| Soul R$_x$ #19 | Be Compassionate | 53 |
| Soul R$_x$ #20 | Forgive | 55 |
| Soul R$_x$ #21 | Love Yourself From The Inside Out | 57 |
| Soul R$_x$ #22 | Each Day Is A Chance to Reset | 59 |
| Soul R$_x$ #23 | Build Strength On The Inside | 61 |
| Soul R$_x$ #24 | Get Out Of Your Own Way | 65 |
| Soul R$_x$ #25 | Remember Yourself | 67 |
| Soul R$_x$ #26 | Be The Gatekeeper Of Your Joy | 69 |

| | | | |
|---|---|---|---|
| Soul R$_x$ #27 | Love Your Body | | 73 |
| Soul R$_x$ #28 | Break Up With Yourself | | 75 |
| Soul R$_x$ #29 | Accept The Compliment | | 77 |

## INSPIRATION

| | | | |
|---|---|---|---|
| Soul R$_x$ #30 | Create and Hold The Space For Inspiration | | 81 |
| Soul R$_x$ #31 | Be The Inspiration | | 83 |
| Soul R$_x$ #32 | Be An Encourager | | 85 |
| Soul R$_x$ #33 | Dance With Wonder | | 87 |
| Soul R$_x$ #34 | Be An Influential Energy Source | | 89 |
| Soul R$_x$ #35 | Make Mental Movies | | 91 |
| Soul R$_x$ #36 | Create A Starting Point For Your Dreams | | 93 |
| Soul R$_x$ #37 | You Are Not Alone | | 95 |
| Soul R$_x$ #38 | Be Enthusiastic | | 97 |
| Soul R$_x$ #39 | Be A Living Work Of Art | | 99 |
| Soul R$_x$ #40 | Free Up Mental Space | | 101 |
| Soul R$_x$ #41 | Own Your Dreams | | 103 |

## CONNECTION

| | | | |
|---|---|---|---|
| Soul R$_x$ #42 | Separate Your Godly Messages From Your Egoic Messages | | 107 |
| Soul R$_x$ #43 | Check In With Yourself | | 109 |
| Soul R$_x$ #44 | Allow Nature To Teach You | | 111 |
| Soul R$_x$ #45 | Listen With Purpose | | 113 |
| Soul R$_x$ #46 | Have Meaningful Conversations | | 115 |
| Soul R$_x$ #47 | Use The Power Of Your Breath | | 117 |
| Soul R$_x$ #48 | Seek A Circle of Like Minded People | | 119 |
| Soul R$_x$ #49 | Reclaim Time For Personal Connection | | 121 |
| Soul R$_x$ #50 | Take The Spiritual High Road | | 123 |
| Soul R$_x$ #51 | Protect Your Peace | | 125 |
| Soul R$_x$ #52 | Listen To The Longing | | 129 |
| Soul R$_x$ #53 | Everyone Needs To Belong | | 131 |

## GREATNESS

| | | | |
|---|---|---|---|
| Soul R$_x$ #54 | Take Responsibility For Your Life | | 135 |
| Soul R$_x$ #55 | Create A Compelling Vision For Your Life | | 137 |

| | | |
|---|---|---:|
| Soul R$_x$ #56 | Tell A New Story | 139 |
| Soul R$_x$ #57 | Remove Limiting Beliefs | 141 |
| Soul R$_x$ #58 | Get In The Game | 145 |
| Soul R$_x$ #59 | There Are Many Paths To Greatness | 147 |
| Soul R$_x$ #60 | Choose Your Dream Life | 149 |
| Soul R$_x$ #61 | Live In A State Of Great Expectation | 151 |
| Soul R$_x$ #62 | Step Into Your Greatness | 153 |
| Soul R$_x$ #63 | Put Down The Heavy Baggage | 155 |
| Soul R$_x$ #64 | There Is No Cap On Your Potential | 157 |
| Soul R$_x$ #65 | Intensity Reveals Your Brilliance | 159 |

## MINDSET

| | | |
|---|---|---:|
| Soul R$_x$ #66 | You Are The Company You Keep | 163 |
| Soul R$_x$ #67 | Validate All Experiences | 165 |
| Soul R$_x$ #68 | Positive Thinking Is A Practice | 169 |
| Soul R$_x$ #69 | A Mind Shift Is A Life Shift | 171 |
| Soul R$_x$ #70 | Opt Out Of Drama | 173 |
| Soul R$_x$ #71 | Always Do Your Best | 175 |
| Soul R$_x$ #72 | Create Your Story | 177 |
| Soul R$_x$ #73 | See The Beauty In Every Day | 179 |
| Soul R$_x$ #74 | Use The Opportunities That Lie Before You | 181 |
| Soul R$_x$ #75 | Reframe Failure | 183 |

## AUTHENTICITY

| | | |
|---|---|---:|
| Soul R$_x$ #76 | Be Authentic | 187 |
| Soul R$_x$ #77 | Achieve Authentic Connection | 189 |
| Soul R$_x$ #78 | Know What You Value | 191 |
| Soul R$_x$ #79 | Trade Happiness For Fulfillment | 197 |
| Soul R$_x$ #80 | Refrain From Attaching Yourself to Labels | 199 |
| Soul R$_x$ #81 | Practice Yourself Into Being | 201 |
| Soul R$_x$ #82 | Develop A Spiritual Practice | 203 |
| Soul R$_x$ #83 | Be Vulnerable | 205 |
| Soul R$_x$ #84 | Make Decisions With Your Internal Committee | 207 |
| Soul R$_x$ #85 | Bring Purpose To Your Life | 209 |

## CELEBRATION

| | | |
|---|---|---|
| Soul R$_x$ #86 | Bookend Your Day With Thanks | 213 |
| Soul R$_x$ #87 | Enjoy Where You Are Right Now | 215 |
| Soul R$_x$ #88 | Honour Yourself | 217 |
| Soul R$_x$ #89 | Do Things That Make You Feel Good | 219 |
| Soul R$_x$ #90 | Transform Routine Into Ritual | 221 |
| Soul R$_x$ #91 | Celebrate Ordinary | 223 |

## POWER

| | | |
|---|---|---|
| Soul R$_x$ #92 | Learn To Take The Losses Without Getting Defeated | 227 |
| Soul R$_x$ #93 | Develop An Inner Coach | 229 |
| Soul R$_x$ #94 | Become Patient | 231 |
| Soul R$_x$ #95 | Minimize Worrying | 233 |
| Soul R$_x$ #96 | Words Matter | 235 |
| Soul R$_x$ #97 | Use Mother Nature To Heal You | 237 |
| Soul R$_x$ #98 | Develop A Sense Of Humour | 239 |
| Soul R$_x$ #99 | Remove the Excuses | 241 |
| Soul R$_x$ #100 | Make A Decision | 243 |
| Soul R$_x$ #101 | Assume Nothing | 247 |

## BONUS SOUL PRESCRIPTIONS

| | | |
|---|---|---|
| Soul R$_x$ #102 | Face Your Fears | 251 |
| Soul R$_x$ #103 | Be Open | 253 |
| Soul R$_x$ #104 | Detach Yourself From The Outcome | 255 |

| | |
|---|---|
| Acknowledgements | 257 |
| About the Author | 259 |

# Foreword

What is success and how is it measured?

Many people believe that success is measured solely by monetary gains, but as Dana Lloyd so beautifully writes, it is about finding your happiness and living from that space.

*Soul Prescription 101 Ways to Find Joy, Meaning and Fulfillment* is a guide to finding your purpose and thriving by using all the tools she provides. I loved reading her personal stories and felt inspired by her words of wisdom. She takes you on her journey of letting go of all the attachments that were holding her back and in doing so helps the reader let go of their attachments as well.

I highly recommend her book.

Skye Dyer

# My Journey

On the morning of October 26, 1988 my life and my mother's life changed forever. The phone rang. From the hallway, I watched my mother casually walk across the kitchen to answer the telephone. She answered with her standard "Hello?" Within moments, all colour drained from her face. She erupted into tears. I had just witnessed my mother receiving the jarring news that her mother had died of a heart attack while on a shopping trip. My mother's life changed forever because at age thirty six, she had lost her last parent. My life changed forever too because my grandmother's passing launched within me a deep curiosity about life and death. It prompted a lot of questions to which I could not find any answers.

At my grandmother's wake, I remember standing by her casket staring at her body. I was looking at an empty shell. I leaned in to kiss her one last time. She was cold. There was no one receiving the kiss. I pulled my face from hers. As I stared at her, I thought where did *she* go? Where did the Essence go that powered her inspiration, her creativity, her laughter, her insight, her thoughts? Where did *that* go? What was *that?* At sixteen, I did not know how to answer this or even know who to ask. With no obvious answers in sight, my busy teenage life quieted my unanswered questions. The questions about that Essence would go dormant for now, but my curiosity about it did not. At sixteen, curious and introspective, something had been activated inside me. I did not know it yet, but this was the point I had become a seeker.

Life moved on. With my big life questions still quietly lurking in the background, I graduated high school and university, married and found a job that paid the bills. I superficially moved through life. I worked for five years before questions began to bubble up inside me again. Not about death this time, but about life. I was feeling unsettled. Was I meant to be doing what I was doing? I graduated as a teacher, but I was not teaching. Was that the problem? I liked the company I worked for, but I began not enjoying my work. There was nothing fulfilling about what I was doing. It was a job that paid the bills. I started to feel confused. I had a good paying job, responsibility, good feedback on my work and I worked with nice people, yet something nagged at me. Was this what I was supposed to be doing for the rest of my life? Working in a cubicle waiting to receive pins honouring years of service? Was I making a mountain out of a molehill? Did everyone else feel this way and just sucked it up? Is this what life really was? Is this what adulthood looked like? Pretending to be a grown up when I was a kid was way more fun than this. I was beginning to have a hard time accepting this was my fate AND I wanted to know from where was this constant barrage of questioning coming? I felt something was out of alignment, but I did not have an inkling as to how I was going to figure it out.

I knew one thing for sure. It was time to shift gears. My husband and I decided to start a family *because having a baby makes life so much easier.* I made the decision to leave my job to become a stay at home mom to my son. The purposeless feeling disappeared for awhile displaced by the demands of motherhood. Eventually the big question found me again. "What was I really supposed to be doing with my life?" *Really?* This question was still bugging me. I gave birth to another human being. What could be more fulfilling than that? Was this not enough purpose in my life? When I held a traditional role in the corporate world, the question arose. When I held a traditional motherly role, the question arose. There was no escaping it. There was a thread of unhappiness weaving its way through my life. Clearly my outward life was not having a positive impact on my happiness.

I did sometimes try to face the BIG question, "What was I supposed to be doing with my life?" Well, sort of. When the question came up, I stared it down like we were in a gun duel in the Wild West until I could not take it anymore. I always looked away losing the battle. I could not stand the question staring at me all judgemental like I was supposed to know what the answer was. It would take me the better part of a decade before I began to realize that the repeated question bubbling up, 'What am I really supposed to be doing with my life?' was coming from somewhere, but from where was the source of this nudging?

I did a lot of soul searching, reading, reflecting, got coached, became a Life Coach and listened to others. I eventually came to the conclusion I had two journeys to take in my lifetime. One was to find out what I was to DO in my life. I was fiercely determined to find the answer. As I slowly shifted my life toward activities I loved, I landed on a path of coaching, training, writing, and speaking. It feels right and is fulfilling and continues to evolve. The second journey I had to take was a spiritual one. The nagging question, "What am I supposed to do with my life?", was a nudge coming from my Soul which I refer to, in this book, as my Highest Self. It was whispering to me all along pushing me to be more. When I stopped resisting the nudge, I came into alignment with it. I felt happier and more hopeful. I felt like I had a greater purpose. I listened to the whisperings of my Soul allowing myself to be guided. Something was powering my thoughts, reflections, inspirations, laughter, and insight just as I had wondered about upon my grandmother's death. I eventually came to realize that the Essence that left my grandmother upon her death was the same Essence that was nudging me to question my life. I was slowly and surely being spiritually awakened.

As part of my purpose, I feel moved to inspire and empower people to create joy, meaning and fulfillment in their lives. I see people struggling in ordinary and extraordinary ways. The ordinary struggles are as equally hard as the extraordinary ones because it is the everyday stuff that is inescapable. Most of the ordinary struggles are inner struggles such as mustering up the courage to say no to others, standing up for yourself, balancing work and family, sticking to choices, being kind to yourself, pushing yourself to achieve goals, or feeling happy. Others have extraordinary challenges like diseases that challenge their bodies, caring for sick loved ones, or suffering great losses. Both ordinary and extraordinary challenges can dilute joy, diminish meaning and deplete fulfillment. I have come to realize that joy, meaning and fulfillment can still be present in your life even if you face challenges.

In a world, where a prescription for *the* magic pill to solve struggles is common, I hope that the ideas contained within this book will give you practical ways of looking at your life. Many times throughout this book I refer to the "Highest Self" which is a term I use to name the Essence that is nudging me. In this book, I have interchangeably used the words Soul, Authentic Self, Essence, Inner Being, Universe or God depending on the context. For me, all the terms speak to the same powerful force to which everyone has the ability to connect. The terms are less significant than the force itself. My spiritual journey is to stay in alignment with my Highest Self. This is the place from which I choose to operate in my human experience. Falling out of alignment with my Highest Self is a part of the human condition. The disconnection is needed in order to appreciate everything that my Highest Self has to offer. It only takes feeling badly, the terrible feeling of worry or a taste of fear to quickly awaken me to my spiritual status. I am not willing to stay in a state of negativity for long, quickly seeking the comfort of my Highest Self.

Life is a combination of doing and being. The prescriptions contained within these pages are practical ways I have learned to align with my Highest Self. These Soul Prescriptions are meant to enrich your life and to gain depth from your experiences. Live your life consciously. Go through life in an awakened state. You have more power and control over your human experience than you think you do. You have the power to create your own joy, meaning and fulfillment and you have a beautiful life in which to do it.

## *The Inner Critic*

I love being aligned with my Highest Self. It is the relationship with my Inner Being that allows me to be authentic, joyful and purposeful. There is so much joy when I am aligned with it, but there is another force that exists within me, my Inner Critic. The Inner Critic is part of the Ego. It has the power to lure me from my Highest Self and ultimately my Joy if I allow it.

I wish I could tell you why the Ego exists. My best guess? Perhaps protection. If you were born in ancient times, your Ego would have served a primal role. A fight or flight response would kick in if you were in danger. In modern times, the Ego serves to protect you too; for example, think about when you meet someone for the first time who you want to date. Are you showing up authentically? Do you pretend to like things you do not? Or speak in a different tone? Or act differently than normal? The Ego is at play protecting you. You want to be liked. Think about when you have had a job interview. Did you behave or speak differently? Exaggerate your abilities? The Ego is at play protecting you. You want to be chosen.

When you use the Ego as protection, however, you are not playing in the space of your Highest Self. You are playing scared. And a big reason why you play scared is thanks, in part, to your Inner Critic. It is the other voice in your head that fabricates stories, makes assumptions, passes judgement, makes you worried, fires up jealousy, or makes you think you are not good enough.

Allow me to introduce you to my Inner Critic. She is a gal named Roz. She never really goes away, so in order to tame her, I had to name her. Roz goes everywhere with me. I imagine Roz, as she rides shotgun with me in the car, wearing a flowery dress that covers her robust figure while her puffy, unruly, blond curly hair rests against the passenger seat headrest. Her feet dressed in bright pink rubber boots are propped up on the dash of the car. One arm lies across her chest providing a resting spot for the other arm so she can casually smoke a cigarette. If I am playing small, her voice stays small, but her voice is filled with just enough judgemental comments to keep the insecurities and anxiousness alive within me. When I want to play big, she plays big. Her voice gets loud and critical, especially when I want to do something important in my life: get in shape, eat better, grow my business, speak in public, change direction, or try anything new. She always seems to have a reason why it is not a good idea or why I am not good enough.

As fierce protector of my joy, I keep Roz in her place. It is my job to stay in alignment with my Highest Self. I do my best to turn down Roz's voice so I can hear the one that serves me best. I refer to the Inner Critic often throughout this book. Once you become aware of this voice, you can do something about it. More importantly, you will realize that you are not the negative voice of your Inner Critic. You and your Inner Critic are not one and the same. You have the power to choose which voice to give your attention. Do you want to give all your attention to your Inner Critic which can make you feel badly and keeps you from getting the most from life OR do you want to pay more attention to your Highest Self? Your choice.

Name your Inner Critic so you can manage it.

What is the name of your Inner Critic?

*"When you live unconsciously, you drift from your Highest Self."*

## Soul R<sub>x</sub> #1

## *Relentlessly Seek Your Highest Self*

Consider that you are a spiritual being having a human experience. Consider that there is a Highest Self that exists within you as well as an Ego. These two parts of you exist as part of your spiritual journey. The Highest Self is a powerful and divine force that allows you to give birth to all that you want and everything you want to be. The Ego is the smaller, petty human self that draws you away from your Highest Self. The Ego is not to be dismissed as it serves a very important role in showing you what you do not want. It helps push you to align with your Highest Self; for example, when fear is too much, sadness too deep, the feelings of worry too intense, you surrender and move to the space of comfort, your Highest Self.

Everything that your Highest Self has to offer makes you feel so good that you are not willing to be anywhere else other than being positive, being kind, being responsible for yourself, feeling connected, etc. The gap between your Highest Self and how you show up in life is the measure of your spiritual journey. The bigger the gap, the larger the spiritual journey. The speed at which you shift back to your Highest Self is a sign of your spiritual maturity.

Each day you take a spiritual journey. Each day presents you with the opportunity to be aligned with your Highest Self. Where are you on your journey today? This is powerful information. Are you sliding toward what feels good or sliding toward what does NOT feel good? Moving toward what does not feel good is moving out of alignment with your Highest Self. How long are you willing to be out of alignment with your Highest Self?

# Spiritual Scale

⟵⎯⎯⎯⎯⎯⎯⎯⎯⎯⎯⎯⎯⎯⎯⎯⎯⎯⎯⟶

| **Highest Self** | **Ego** |
|---|---|
| Authenticity | Fake |
| Joy | Misery |
| Peace | Annoyed |
| Love | Hate |
| Gratitude | Complaining |
| Fulfillment | Emptiness |
| Excellence | Perfection |
| Creativity | Worry |
| Freedom | Jealous |
| Worthy | Fear |
| Present | Past/ Future |
| Inspiration | Anxious |
| Connection | Separation |
| Trust | Unworthiness |
| Faith | Insecurity |
| Expectation | Judgement |
| Imagination | Disconnected |
| Possibility | Limited |
| Understanding | Offended |

When you live unconsciously, you drift from your Highest Self. Every moment of every day you are either moving toward joy or moving away from it. You can move back and forth on the Spiritual Scale. Your greatest spiritual practice is staying connected to your Highest

Self. Notice how often you get detached from your Highest Self. Perhaps you get cut off in traffic, someone says a snide remark to you or you are waiting too long in a grocery store line. Become conscious of your drifting. Practice catching yourself out of alignment then practice shifting yourself back into alignment with your Highest Self.

People spend a lot of time and money seeking all that the Highest Self has always been holding for them. The shift back to your Highest Self is a shift back to the present moment. It is an easy shift that costs you nothing. The journey to your Highest Self is free. You can move back to that peaceful space by: choosing better feeling thoughts, speaking kindly to yourself, dropping assumptions, choosing not to have an argument, choosing not to be right, giving yourself a pep talk, giving yourself a peace talk, practicing love, practicing kindness, expressing gratitude. There are many ways to get and stay there. The most important element is the practice of doing it. It is conscious living 101. The power is in the practice.

All that your Highest Self has to offer is only a small shift away. Wanting to be connected to your Highest Self is wanting better for yourself, so you can live your most powerful life.

Where are you on the spiritual scale right now?

# *GROWTH*

*"You are already good enough."*

## Soul R$_x$ #2

## *Growth, Not Self-Improvement*

A few years ago, I signed up for a meditation course. As I plunked myself down next to a friend, she turned to me and fired off a list of rhetorical questions, "Why are we doing this? Why are we always self-improving? Why are we never satisfied with ourselves?" I politely agreed with her, but felt a bit sheepish or maybe I was slightly offended because I felt self-improvement was exactly my lane as a coach and a teacher. I help people be better, do better, think better. What was wrong with that?

Later that evening, my friend's questions repeatedly looped in my head like a news ticker tape moving across the bottom of a television screen. What was bothering me about the question, "Why are we always self-improving?" As I reflected on it, a light bulb went on. I realized the words "self-improvement" had a negative undertone. Even my friend used the words "self-improvement" exasperatingly. No wonder. Self-improvement suggests there is something wrong with you. The words speak to you from a point of less than.

I also realized I am not in the self-improvement lane. I am in the growth industry acting as a catalyst encouraging people to get engaged in their lives. Growing is based on the premise "you are already good enough". You do not have to struggle to get to good enough. You are already there AND life is richer when you choose to grow.

Believe you are already whole; you are not broken. Broken is only a perspective manifested by your Ego to diminish you keeping you from your best life. You have everything you need right now. Think of a tree, it cannot choose to stop growing; it cannot help but grow to its potential. It never gets to a point where it says, "I'm done. This is as far as I am going." As long as it continues to use the resources it is given: air, water, sun, soil, it continues to grow. Use everything you have to grow. You are resourceful.

You are good enough. Focus on growing, not self-improving.

In what area of your life, would you most like to grow?

*"Start your day with a dose of soul food."*

## *Soul R$_x$ #3*

## *Nourish Your Mind Daily*

One of my morning rituals involves having breakfast. My body speaks to me in hunger. As soon as I eat something, I am recharged to think, concentrate, and work more effectively. If I do not eat, I feel lethargic or foggy. I know when I need to nourish my physical body because it gives me signals I cannot ignore. Your mind also signals for you to be fed.

How do you know when it is time to nourish your mind?

- When you find yourself not in the present moment; for example, you may be in your morning shower thinking of your day ahead instead of enjoying the water running over your body.
- When you are paying more attention to the negative voice in your head, rerunning its recordings derailing you from joy and keeping you from your Highest Self.
- When you get locked in needless battles with others.
- When you are stressed.
- When you think about work/life balance and how you have none.
- When you possess a negative attitude.
- When you engage in gossip.
- When you feel paralyzed by decisions.
- When worry has become your default state.

Just as you understand that a rumbling stomach means hunger, learn the signs that your mind is hungry.

To feed your mind:

- Read something motivational such as a passage from your favourite author or book.
- Set the intention for the day. Purposefully indicate what you want your day to look like.
- Meditate.
- Do yoga.
- Express gratitude.
- Remind yourself. Place an uplifting quote on the bathroom mirror before you go to bed so you see it first thing in the morning. It is amazing what a little reminder will do.
- Journal.
- Reset your attitude.
- Practice bringing awareness to moments in your day.
- Go out of your way to express kindness.

When you choose to nourish your mind, you are engaging your Highest Self. Put your Highest Self in charge, otherwise your Ego will execute a hostile takeover running your day like a drunken sailor. Moving through your day connected to your Highest Self increases the quality of your day and sets you up to experience joy.

Start your day with a dose of soul food.

How will you feed your mind today?

*"Letting go is an act of self-love."*

## Soul R$_x$ #4

## *Let Go*

When you hold onto an idea, a belief, a relationship, or a job, you can become shackled by security, certainty, comfortableness, recognition or status. Holding on can be costly, especially when you know that something no longer serves you.

Holding on to :

- friendships that do not serve you, may be keeping you from meeting your best friend for life.
- a dead marriage fearing an uncertain future, may keep you from the one real love of your life.
- the fear of accidents prevents you from adventure.
- your current job fearing that you may fail if you take a new opportunity, keeps you from growing.

Holding on is paralyzing. It keeps you in a holding pattern distancing you from getting what you want. Letting go frees you from the ties that bind bringing flow back into your life paying you huge dividends in the form of new experiences, fresh perspectives, and dynamic people. Shift from viewing change as hard to change is refreshing.

Letting go is:

- courageous because you must move past your fear in order to make changes.
- healing because you release what is causing you pain.

- trusting because in the face of uncertainty you expect your best life still lies ahead.
- freeing because you relinquish control without always knowing how everything will go.
- spiritual because "letting go" is a practice. The more you do it, the better you get at it. A spiritual practice is what you adopt to bring you to your highest good. The speed at which you let go is directly proportional to your spiritual growth.

It is time to let go. Let go of the limiting beliefs, negative self-talk, other people who do not serve you, fear of failure, fear of success, rejection, not being good enough, preconceived notions, unsatisfactory situations. When you let go and let change happen, you are sending out a request for happiness, fulfillment, meaning, richness. Letting go is an act of self-love releasing you from bondage moving you toward freedom.

What do you need to let go?

*"Being uncomfortable is a sign that a growth opportunity is present."*

## Soul R$_x$ #5

## *Get Comfortable With Being Uncomfortable*

Two years ago I decided to learn golf. I never played any sport in my life or even watched sports, so I was starting from scratch. I joined golf because I joked with our kids that my husband and I would be golfing in Florida when we retire, so that is where they can expect to visit us in our golden years. It occurred to me one day that if I actually wanted to play golf when I am older, I might want to learn it now. I decided to join my local Golf Club.

I really did not expect the learning curve. For the first six weeks I tried to learn the game based on tips from my husband and other golfers. To play more, I joined ladies night at the golf course. If you've ever had to stand before a crowd of people to tee off when you really do not know how to play, it is daunting. As you approach the tee, it feels like you are walking toward a guillotine. There is a crowd of people watching you. They do not care how you play, but I cared...a lot! If I had a terrible drive, I would look back at the women standing around, slightly embarrassed mumbling, "I'm new," trying to explain my game. I wondered how long I could use that excuse.

Learning golf taught me lessons in vulnerability and perseverance. If I wanted to truly learn how to play, I had to be vulnerable enough to stay uncomfortable and persevere through my discomfort. I had to get comfortable with being uncomfortable. I was uncomfortable with not knowing how to play. I was uncomfortable with people watching me learn. I was uncomfortable making mistakes. I was uncomfortable playing with strangers which often happens when you play golf. If I wanted to learn this game so I can play golf in Florida in my retirement years, being uncomfortable was an idea I had to embrace. I continued to play regardless of how uncomfortable I felt. I have lots of room for growth, but now I can easily play a round of golf with friends and colleagues. Mission accomplished.

Being uncomfortable is a sign that a growth opportunity is present. To get more out of life, growth is inevitable. Growth is uncomfortable. If you can persevere through it, you grow immensely. Growing takes courage because it requires you to be vulnerable. Never miss an opportunity to grow because you are unwilling to show your vulnerability.

What makes you uncomfortable?

*"Playing in your strength zone is like turbo-boost for your Soul."*

## Soul R<sub>x</sub> #6

## *Know Your Strengths*

Both personal and spiritual growth are about expansion. Knowing your strengths is a way for you to grow and expand in this world. People often spend time focusing on their weaknesses, however, improving upon what you are not good at is wasted energy. By focusing on your weaknesses, you may be able to improve marginally, but not significantly. Your strength zone is where you can soar. Your strength zone is where you have impact. You achieve excellence when you deploy your strengths.

You want to excel in life? Focus on what you do well. Identify your strengths by answering these questions:

- What have you been told you do well?
- What are you doing when people are impressed by you?
- What skill or quality makes you shine?
- What do you know you are good at?
- What are you doing when you feel energized and time flies?
- What would you do even if you did not get paid?
- What are you doing when you are feeling inspired?

Strengths may not be specific such as "I am good at selling." What you may actually be great at is connecting with people. You could use that strength to lead at work or organize a charity or be a public speaker. What you do is not as important as who you are. Slowly shift to applying your strengths more often in your work and in your life. Note the difference.

Operating from your strength zone has the ability to transform your life. Your enjoyment level rises. You feel more connected to yourself. You will get more positive feedback from others. You will find new ways of using your strengths which creates more opportunities. You will get called upon to use your strengths because using your strengths makes you stand out.

Furthermore, when you connect to what makes you strong in life, you are aligned with your Highest Self. You are meant to feel good and do good in this life. Using your strengths is a way for you to do that. Strengths multiply your impact. Playing in your strength zone is like turbo-boost for your Soul. You can expand and grow more quickly when you are doing what brings you to life. Connecting with your strengths is using your life in the best possible way.

What are your top three strengths?

*"Stop doing the things that hold you back, so you can start doing the things that move you forward."*

## Soul R<sub>x</sub> #7

## Stop It

Years ago I watched a comedy sketch that involved a woman having a counselling session with her psychologist. The scene opened with the woman describing her fear of being buried alive in a box. Her psychologist quickly concludes she is claustrophobic. He says he knows exactly what advice to give her. The client gets her notebook ready to write down the good doctor's wisdom. Her psychologist assures her that the advice will be easy to remember. It is just two words. She leans in to hear the advice and her doctor leans forward too, then yells, "Stop It!" She is taken aback by his simple advice yet reluctantly accepts it. She then continues to list other issues she has difficulty with and each time her psychologist yells "Stop It!"

It is a very funny sketch highlighting simple advice: Stop It. Not all issues are so easily solved with such simplistic instruction; however, there are many things you do unconsciously every day that you could stop doing which would dramatically improve the quality of your life.

| | |
|---|---|
| Criticizing yourself and others. | *Stop It.* |
| Gossiping. | *Stop It.* |
| Spending money foolishly. | *Stop It.* |
| Wanting to be liked. | *Stop It.* |
| Wondering what other people think. | *Stop It.* |
| Delaying decisions. | *Stop It.* |
| Succumbing to your fears. | *Stop It.* |
| Needing other people's opinions to make decisions. | *Stop It.* |

Waiting for things to be perfect to begin.     *Stop It.*
Waiting for the right time to begin.           *Stop It.*
Looking for permission or validation.          *Stop It.*
Obsessing over your smart phones.              *Stop It.*

Stopping has the power to change your life. Stopping behaviours slows negative momentum, removes you from old pathways, and jolts you out of bad habits. Stop doing the things that hold you back so you can start doing the things that move you forward.

What do you need to stop doing today?

*"Starting is a nod to the Universe that you are ready to receive."*

## Soul R$_x$ #8

## Start It

It is easy to get in a rut. If you want a new direction or change in your life, you need to start taking action. Doing something different, anything, is the simplest way to move in a new direction. Putting yourself in action mode gets you unstuck and builds momentum. Action may be internal or external.

**Internal Starts:**

*Start* developing beliefs that work for you.
*Start* having a better attitude.
*Start* encouraging yourself and others.
*Start* talking more kindly to yourself.
*Start* finding reasons why you can.
*Start* seeing possibility.
*Start* taking inventory of abundance in your life.

**External Starts:**

*Start* making the phone calls you need to make.
*Start* with one step toward the dream that is eating you up inside.
*Start* eating better.
*Start* moving more.
*Start* a new hobby.
*Start* a new group.
*Start* living the life you want.
*Start* having the conversations you want to have.

A beautiful thing happens when you start any new change. You have emitted a signal that you want something to be different for you. Starting is a nod to the Universe that you are ready to receive. Starting activates your Highest Self to operate on your behalf. Things begin lining up for you. It might not be obvious for a while, but eventually the right people and opportunities begin showing up. It is magical when that happens. Even more magical is when you realize it.

Do not let starting scare you. Starting any change can feel hard in the beginning. Heading to the gym for the first time in ten years might feel uncomfortable. Your first push-up might feel like you have two people sitting on your back. Starting the business you've always wanted may feel overwhelming. Shifting to recognizing what's working in your life might feel foreign. Stick with your starts.

Make starting easy. Your biggest dreams or problems can be broken into small bites. The most important part of the process is to start taking the bites. How do you eat an elephant? One bite at a time. Start and keep it simple. Anything can be achieved if you break it down into small enough bites. You might be waiting on life to change, but rather life is waiting on you.

What do you need to start doing today?

*"Learning from adversity is leveraging the human experience."*

## Soul R<sub>x</sub> #9

## Learn From Adversity

Adversity is a part of life. Remember what happens to one, happens to us all. A life is not exempt from challenge. Adversity is like sandpaper. It is irritating and creates a lot of friction. Just as sandpaper is used to transform a piece of wood, adversity is used to transform lives. If you allow it, it can change you for the better. Step back and view the adversity from an objective standpoint. Instead of wanting this situation less, use it to discover more about you. What has it taught you? How can you use this situation to refine your desires, your thinking, your attitude, your beliefs, and your values? Learning from adversity is leveraging the human experience.

Adversity does not come to take you down. It comes to show you what you do not want. People complain about living in challenging times, but inside every challenge lies opportunity. There are always financial opportunities inside economic challenges, an opportunity to change when you feel stuck, an opportunity to meet new people when you feel lonely, an opportunity to influence when you feel like situations have become immoveable, and an opportunity to find peace in the midst of chaos. When you can find the seed of goodness within adversity, you are aligned with your Highest Self. Do not ask, "Why Me?" ask, "What's next?" "What should I be learning here?" When you suffer a setback, give it minor awareness then shift quickly to what you want to happen and focus your energy there. This is spiritual maturity.

Adversity is *the* greatest teacher. No matter the situation, it will pass, but before it does, grab the lesson contained within it. Use adversity to push you toward your goals not farther away from them.

What has adversity taught you?

*"When you are not living a life of resonance,
it is an indicator to change something."*

## Soul R$_x$ #10

## *Know When To Change*

Resonance is your internal spiritual barometer. Living a life of resonance indicates that you are on the right path; however, when you are no longer living a life of resonance, it is an indicator to change something.

You know if...

- what you do for a living resonates with you or not.
- who you spend time with resonates with you or not.
- how you spend your time resonates with you or not.
- how you spend your money resonates with you or not.

Pay attention and trust that your Inner Being knows more than your Outer Being. People tend to do things longer than they intended, for example, stay in relationships long after they are over, hold onto jobs that no longer fulfill them, or volunteer when the opportunity no longer satisfies them. When you no longer feel resonance, it is time to change.

Understanding resonance is like playing the childhood game of *Hot or Cold*. An object is hidden in a room. The player tasked with finding the hidden object closes her eyes moving around the room based on verbal clues given by another player. If she is nowhere near the object, she is given the clue "cold." When the player moves closer to the hidden object, the clue "warmer" is given. When the player moves extremely close to the object, the player providing the clues yells "hot!" Living a life of resonance is like this game. Constantly move toward what you want. Go to where "hot" is. Playing a real life game of *Hot or Cold* brings you into alignment with all that you want.

Know that you can change direction in your life. Do what brings you joy. When something resonates with you, you may experience goose bumps or get excited or passionate. Stay alert to both the physical and emotional signs of resonance. Your Highest Self is speaking to you showing you a path. When you feel the signs, ask yourself, what about this situation is resonating with me?

Pay attention to resonance. Know when it is time to change.

What is not resonating in your life?

*"When you walk away from perfection, you walk back to worthiness."*

## Soul R$_x$ #11

## *Make Excellence Your Standard, Not Perfection*

I joke that I am a recovering perfectionist. What is not a joke is the angst and internal conflict my perfectionism has caused me through the years. The first time I can recall being aware of perfectionism occurred in grade two. I have an image ingrained in my mind of my seven year old self sitting in a small chair with elbows propped up on a white topped desk, my small hands gripping my report card. My eyes were drawn to the bottom of the page where the teacher put a checkmark beside the word "conscientious" to describe me. I remember thinking, "Oh, no. I am conscientious." Without even knowing what it meant, I remember not liking that description, so I asked the teacher for clarification. I remember getting the sense it was a good thing, but not a great thing. Conscientious was a loaded word. I know now it was perfectionism rearing its ugly head, but there was not a box for that word. I was meticulous, but I obsessed over getting things right. There was a reason I wanted to get things right. Wanting to get things right and doing things right was motivation for validation. Being validated by the teacher became the measuring stick of worthiness. In my young mind, a good student equalled being a good person. Academic achievement became a way to feel worthy. Conscientiousness, however, masked perfection. Perfection eventually became a heavy backpack I carried everywhere feeling like I could not put it down, not even for a second. It felt like the world was holding me hostage when in fact it was only me.

Perfection is a wedge separating you from your Highest Self. Striving for perfection knocks you out of alignment with your Highest Self.

**Perfection** prevents you from getting started or pursuing your big ideas. When perfection becomes your standard, beginning becomes overwhelming. You will question whether you should even attempt a goal in the first place. You set yourself up for defeat before you begin. Goals, through the lens of perfection, appear as insurmountable mountains.

**Excellence** as a standard says I can begin while doing my best. Walking away from perfection allows you to find an easy point of entry into your goals.

**Perfection** plays into your fears of not being good enough. "If I can't get it right, why bother even trying?" When you walk away from perfection, you walk back to worthiness.

**Excellence** is acceptance that you are good enough and that doing your best is enough.

**Perfection** damages your self-esteem. If you have an idea that you believe is "perfect" and someone does not agree with it, then what? Will you adjust to how the other person believes it should be? Perfection forces you to live according to external influences always reacting to please people. Shift to pleasing yourself. What makes you fulfilled and satisfied? What does that look like?

**Excellence** is an internal standard that is not dependent on the opinions and judgements of others. Your best is enough.

**Perfection** will exhaust you. When you pursue perfection, your goal will always be slightly out of reach. The target always seems to move as you draw closer to it. When is the project finished? When is the dance perfected? When is the song done? Perfection moves the finish line. If the finish line is always moving, perfection will wear you out.

**Excellence** allows for mistakes. There is no need to fret over "getting it right" as there is no "right" outcome. It is the outcome that satisfies you.

**Perfection** robs you of your joy. Perfection lures you away from your Highest Self. It is difficult to experience joy when you are in a state of constantly reaching for a moving target or paralyzed to act because you are afraid to disappoint others.

**Excellence** exists in the same space as joy. They are found together. Get your joy back by giving up perfection.

**Perfection** is an excuse not to be seen in this world. You may tell the world you are not doing something because you are waiting for the right conditions, the right information or the right time, but you know better. Perfection stops you from showing up.

**Excellence** allows you to be seen. "I am willing to stand out while doing my best" or "I am afraid, but I am doing it anyway." "I do not know how to do this, but I am willing to do it imperfectly first." Being seen requires vulnerability. Be seen.

Establish excellence as your new standard. When you align yourself with excellence, you come into alignment with your Highest Self which allows you to live from the same space as freedom, peace and joy. Unshackle yourself from perfection.

What will developing a standard of excellence do for you?

*"Reflection gives your experiences depth."*

## Soul R$_x$ #12

## *Use Reflection To Grow You*

Reflection is a powerful tool you can use to increase awareness around your life. It is a magnifying glass to carefully inspect the details of your experiences. With age, does not necessarily come wisdom. Wisdom is birthed out of reflection. If you want to grow in your life, reflect on your experiences.

**Reflection gives your experiences depth.** Move beyond the surface experience to reveal what that experience taught you. At first glance, an experience may seem to offer you nothing, but magnifying the situation always reveals the take away. Experiences have layers. Examine your experiences from different angles. What was easy about this? What was challenging? What did I learn? What am I grateful for as a result of the situation? How did this challenge my values? How did this emotionally impact me? What am I going to do differently? If you want true insight and wisdom, use your experiences, the good, the bad and the ugly to grow you. Growth formula:

$$\text{Growth} = \text{Experience} + \text{Reflection}$$

**Reflection acts as a measuring stick.** It allows you to measure how you are doing. Reflect on your week, your month, your year. How are you doing compared to where you hoped you would be? What do you need to do to move yourself further along?

**Reflection is a reality check.** When you stare into your experiences, you cannot deny what is looking back. It shows where you truly are on your journey whether it be professionally, financially, emotionally, or spiritually. It is easy to reflect on good experiences, but have the courage to face your difficult experiences too without getting emotionally pulled back into them. Review them objectively like a case study in a textbook.

What would regular reflection do for your growth?

*"When you have more questions than answers, you are embarking on an awakening."*

## Soul R<sub>x</sub> #13

### *Allow the Big Life Questions To Transform You*

At some point, you have or will question life in some way. What I am supposed to be doing with my life? Why can life be so difficult? Why is heartache easier to come by than happiness? What's my purpose? What is the purpose of life? What am I here for? These are big questions. So big that thinking about them makes your head hurt. These questions can be hard to answer. It is easier not to think about them, but when you dodge the big questions, you dodge what life has to offer you. Questions lead you to answers. If the big life questions arise, it means you want more clarity about your life.

I remember buying a booth at a women's event to promote my coaching business when I first became a Life Coach. A Life Coach asks powerful questions such as "If time and money were not an issue, what would you do? When you are at the end of your life, what do you want people to say about you? What must you do in this life to feel fulfilled?" To engage people to talk with me at this event, I typed powerful questions on long, colourful, skinny pieces of construction paper. I stood next to my table grasping them in my hand like a floral arrangement. The pieces of paper drooped like tulips over my clenched fist. As people walked by, I waved my outstretched arm that held my arrangement of powerful questions. I enticed people to talk to me by asking them if they would like one. I was successful in getting many people to stop. They picked a question from the colourful selection. I watched as they read it and showed it to their mom or friend standing beside them. They would laugh aloud not having a clue as to how to respond. Some would say, "Too big. Too big of a question." Some actually handed back the question even though it was a disposable piece of paper. They did not even want the question to be on their person as if they knew it would nag them, sing out to them from their pocket hoping to be answered. These people knew if they spent any time with the chosen question, their reality would be disturbed.

Questions are meant to be catalysts. When you have more questions than answers, you are embarking on an awakening. Questions are the gift of your Highest Self nudging you to pay attention knowing there is more for you to do, more for you to be in this world. Not having the answers is fine. Just begin considering what the answers might be. Questions morph bringing you closer to the solution. One question leads to the next. It might be the next question that turns everything on. The next question might be the one that makes more sense to you allowing you to easily answer it. Allow the questions to flow and you will be moved to the answer. Do not be afraid of questions. Ask more questions, not less.

What questions should you be answering?

# ACCEPTANCE

*"When you fight against your natural unfolding, you are resisting the flow of life."*

## Soul R$_x$ #14

## Be At Peace With The Pace Of Your Unfolding

Everything unfolds at its own pace. Only look to nature to know this truth. Flowers bloom, seasons arrive, the sun rises and sets. Mother Nature is not crossing her fingers hoping spring will arrive this year. It comes. Nature is not in a hurry. Why would your unfolding be any different? You too, are a part of nature's unfolding.

Imagine if you could witness a tree grow or a flower bloom. Minute changes in nature cannot be seen with the naked eye, but they can be captured using time lapse photography. Time lapse is a cinematography technique in which the frequency of the frames are captured at a lower rate than when they are played back. When nature is recorded, this technique makes it possible for you to see life unfold that is too slow for your eyes. It is a reminder that although you may not visibly see the grass grow or flowers bloom, it happens. Your unfolding is like nature.

Nature has an advantage, however. It unfolds minus the worry or anxiousness. Unnecessary stress settles in when you think that you should be somewhere else or doing something more. When you fight against your natural unfolding, you are resisting the flow of life. Remove your resistance by releasing the idea that you are supposed to be somewhere else in your life right now. You are here. There is a saying "go with the flow." It does not mean do whatever everyone else is doing, but to recognize there is a flow to your life, an easiness that exists if you allow it. When you are willing to "go with the flow," you float back to your Highest Self.

The Essence that signals for the flowers to grow is the same one speaking to you. Be at peace with where you are. Listen to your Inner Being that guides you. Find your flow. There is a natural unfolding order in the Universe and you are a part of it. Be at peace with the pace of your unfolding.

What is the most helpful thing you could do to be at peace with your unfolding?

*"When you compare yourself to someone else, you are not honouring YOUR journey."*

## Soul R<sub>x</sub> #15

## *Honour Your Journey*

Comparing yourself to others will steal your joy. You are not in a competition. Before social media, life comparisons were limited to what you saw or heard: your neighbour rolling in their driveway with a new car, a co-worker wearing a doorknob for an engagement ring or overhearing someone's description of their most *amazing* dream vacation in the staff room. Along comes social media to really amplify comparisons. Not only can you see what others have, but now it becomes a status update about how they feel about it. The cherry on top is the cute little emoji that reinforces how they feel in case you did not get it the first time.

In a world driven by social media, everyone's lives, on the surface, look awesome because their Egos are in control of the story. Someone's Ego is telling a story and your Ego is witnessing it. Comparisons come from your Ego. Your Inner Critic spins stories of not having or doing enough or your family pictures are never that perfect or your family does not have game night. Your Ego is in a race, your Highest Self is not.

When you compare yourself to someone else, you are not honouring *your* journey. Comparisons will deplete your happiness, steal your joy, and undermine your worthiness. When you feel yourself becoming jealous, using excuses to explain others lives or wishing you had someone else's life, stuff or journey, you are living life from your Ego. You are giving power to the Inner Critic. Shift into the space of your Highest Self to honour your journey:

- Celebrate and appreciate what you have in your life. Take note of what is working well.

- Celebrate other's joys. (Hint: Connect to your Highest Self before you cruise social media.) A feeling of joy is a feeling of joy whether you are happy for yourself or happy for someone else. Joy is a strong emotion that makes you feel good. Capitalize on the opportunity to use other people's joy to reinforce it in yourself.

Life is a journey, not a race. Drop the comparisons.

What is the most helpful thing you could do to stop comparing yourself to others?

*"Self-acceptance is the gateway to self-love."*

## Soul R<sub>x</sub> #16

## Accept Yourself

Self-acceptance is the gateway to self-love. If you cannot accept who you are, how can you truly love yourself? When you choose not to accept yourself, you are choosing not to see your greatness. It is the recognition of that greatness that will connect you to all that you desire. Do not deny yourself the opportunity to show up fully in this life by turning a blind eye to who you are.

Often what stops you from self-acceptance is your own personal suffering created by your Inner Critic. It does not seem reasonable that you would be birthed into a life of personal suffering. Personal suffering creates a wall that gets built by a collection of negative stories that you have told yourself. The wall will come down when you move to self-acceptance. Personal greatness awaits you on the other side.

You are amazing. Accept and embrace who you are right now. Accept your:

- Gifts and talents
- Preferences
- Quirks
- Body
- Knowledge
- Opinions
- Mistakes
- Interactions
- Choices

- Education
- Background
- Experiences

Love yourself in its entirety. This is 360 degrees of acceptance; nothing is left out. Accepting yourself is the beginning of a new journey leaving yourself open to possibility, change, growth, and learning. Goodness starts showing up in your life when you accept yourself.

What needs to happen to allow you to accept yourself?

*"Acceptance is the spiritual practice of embracing 'what is' right now."*

## Soul R<sub>x</sub> #17

## *You Are Right Where You Are Supposed To Be*

Have you posed this question to yourself, "How did I get to this point in my life?" Perhaps you feel like you have floated aimlessly through life like a piece of driftwood. You easily get anxious or upset thinking you should be farther ahead of where you are; however, you have had a collection of thoughts and experiences that have brought you to this moment. Accept where you are in your life. Wanting your life to be different than what it is creates stress. Acceptance is a spiritual practice of embracing *what is* right now. Acceptance diminishes stress.

Life has unfolded at a pace that you can manage. If you are unsettled where you are, refocus your energy on what you want. Decide where you want to go next. The decision is all yours as you are the co-creator of your own life. You get to decide what's next. Be patient with yourself and with your unfolding.

Which direction do you want to move next?

*LOVE*

*"When you are lost, return to love."*

## Soul R$_x$ #18

## *Love Is The Way*

If there was ever a great ANSWER to everything, it is love. It is life's manifesto. No one can deny the power of love. Everyone wants it because it feels so good. Love is like a ray of sunshine. It is all encompassing. You can feel the warmth of the sun, but you cannot tell where it begins and ends. Like the sun, you know when you are in the warming presence of love. It is a powerful emotion that washes away hate, jealousy, fear, unworthiness and insecurity. Love is powerful.

Love opens the channel to receive what you want in your life. Love is what connects everyone. When tragedy strikes or you gather in celebration of others, love is the great connector that makes you forget your petty woes and join together. You may not speak the same language as others, but people know the invisible force of love because it is more than words. It emanates from you in a touch, look or action. Love links you to another.

You want love? Start emanating it. Love begins with you. Love yourself first. It is your gift to the world. Love yourself, love others, love your experiences. Those who love themselves show up with their light shining so brightly, not only does it shine a light on their own path, it shines a light on other's paths as well.

More importantly, love places you in union with your Highest Self. To withhold love is to separate you from your Highest Self. When you are lost, frustrated, angry or upset, return to love.

Love is the way. Always.

How can you *be* love?

*"Compassion is empathy for how others show up in life, not agreement with what they are doing."*

## Soul R<sub>x</sub> #19

## *Be Compassionate*

The world needs more compassion. Compassion will always be in demand as long as there is human suffering within one person, a group of people, or a country. Everyone is going through something, so be kind and understanding of others.

Suffering does not always look like poverty and helplessness. Suffering might look like worry, stress and fear in your next door neighbour. Suffering may be masked in silence. When people are angry, irritable and unkind, suffering is showing up too. It is easy to overlook suffering in those who disturb other's peace because they invoke negative feelings in others. They tend to get shut out. These people are often the ones who need compassion the most. Often if their bark is loud, their hurt is deep. Be on the lookout for those who need your compassion. Reserve judgement and instead use empathy. Try to see things from the other person's perspective.

Compassion is using the power of the Highest Self. You are a human being having good days and bad days. If you expect to be in receipt of compassion, be generous in giving it to others. Your compassion will always be what someone needed because it says "I see you." People just want to be seen which really means they want to know that they matter. Compassion is empathy for how others show up in life, not agreement with what they are doing.

Demonstrating compassion is your Highest Self in action. Being more compassionate is a heart agreement with your Highest Self which deepens your spiritual growth.

To whom do you need to show compassion?

*"Forgiveness is an act of self-love."*

## Soul R$_x$ #20

## *Forgive*

Forgiveness is for you. To forgive is to open the floodgates to peace. Forgiving is the act of releasing the negative energy held toward another. To not forgive is to loop the same story over and over again allowing the anger and sadness to gain momentum which continues to victimize you. You spend all your time avoiding people who wronged you, using the situation as an excuse not to do something, or allowing yourself to feel terrible all the time. Forgiveness removes the roadblock allowing flow back into your life. Flow might look like friends, connection, love, choice, fulfillment, peace, or happiness.

Withholding forgiveness does not feel good. When I am injured by someone, I get angry. It took me many years (ok…decades) to truly understand the power of forgiveness. I knew I wanted to *be* better. Anger does not serve my highest good. It drags me away from my Highest Self. My spiritual practice now is to move quickly to the space of forgiveness when I feel I have been injured. The more quickly I can return to the space of peace, the more love I have for myself and the more love I have for others. I have resolved to not be a bitter person who holds grudges. By adopting the philosophy that *everyone is on their own journey*, I move to peace more quickly. Practicing forgiveness deepens my spiritual journey. When I see suffering walking up my path, I already know what I must do.

Forgiveness can be challenging, but it is an act of self-love. It is always for you. It does not deny what happened. You cannot change the past, but forgiveness guarantees the event will not steal your future. To choose to forgive says, "I want my joy, peace and power back." It says, "I love myself more than I love victimizing myself." When you are unsure how to love yourself, forgiving is one way to do it.

The power of forgiveness is understated. The uncontrolled stored up negative emotion swirls in your body like a raging storm. To forgive is to bask in the peace after a storm has passed. Forgiveness brings you to personal peace and peace is the language of your Soul.

What would forgiving do for you?

*"Work on your outside because you love yourself, not so you can love yourself."*

## Soul R<sub>x</sub> #21

## *Love Yourself From The Inside Out*

The morning routine is often a reintroduction to the Ego and all its nonsense. As the alarm sounds in the early morning, you get out of bed, walk groggily into the bathroom and catch a glimpse of yourself in the mirror. Your reflection activates your Ego. It has rested all night, but the morning launches the reign of judgment picking up where it left off the night before. You step on the scale and speak unkindly to yourself. You dislike your body, so you scour the internet for the ultimate fitness shortcuts. You do not like your skin, so you slather on expensive skin cream. You do not like your shape, so you hide behind your clothes. The little secret is no matter what you do to the outside, it will not change the inside.

You feed the negative voice when you pay attention to it. The self loathing happens because you believe the negative voice. Believing the Ego is to knowingly enter into an unhealthy relationship. Do not feed your Ego. It is a hungry bully that will leave you lying lifeless on your bathroom floor before your day has begun.

When you get out of bed in the morning, get in alignment with your Highest Self, the quiet voice that is guiding you to be your best. It is always waiting quietly in the background for your return. The negative voice will compete like a noisy toddler for your attention. You can give attention to the Ego or to your Highest Self. The one you feed is the one that wins. Make the shift from listening to your Ego to loving and appreciating yourself. Accept yourself for who you are. Speak kindly to yourself. Cheer yourself on. Encourage yourself by focusing on what you know is going well for you and what you are doing right. These internal actions of love bring you into alignment with your Highest Self.

There is nothing wrong with making yourself look fabulous on the outside, but when it does not match with your Inner Being, there is a disconnect. The inner work of loving yourself pays you great dividends. Once you begin your inside journey, your outside work is authentic. Work on your outside because you love yourself, not so you *can* love yourself.

What can you do to begin loving yourself from the inside out today?

*"Allow your todays to be more important than your yesterdays."*

## Soul R<sub>x</sub> #22

## *Each Day Is A Chance To Reset*

Recognize that no matter what happens today, tomorrow is a new day to begin again.

When I was a young mother, I would collapse on my bed at the end of the day. Some days were like a whirlwind leaving me exhausted. I would lie on my bed staring at the ceiling reviewing the day like a broadcaster reviewing highlights from a sports reel. Some days left me feeling uncertain of my mothering skills and not always proud of how I was showing up. The saving grace was I could fall asleep knowing I could push the reset button in the morning. Each morning was a chance to be better.

People love second chances and every day is a second chance....a chance to be better than yesterday, a chance to move beyond limits, a chance to create a new starting line. Allow your todays to be more important than your yesterdays. Spend little time reliving an experience. It does not serve you. Use what you learned and bring that forward into today. Keep pushing forward.

Hit the reset button and begin again.

In which area of your life do you want to hit the reset button?

*"Confidence is an inside job."*

## Soul R$_x$ #23

## *Build Strength On The Inside*

Confidence is action. Your actions show on the outside how you feel on the inside. If you want to grow in confidence, begin by strengthening your Inner Self, then act. Self-confidence is often used interchangeably or alongside other terms such as self-image and self-esteem. The best explanation I have heard to easily remember what these terms mean were described as:

Self-Image = what you **think** about yourself
Self-Esteem = how you **feel** about yourself
Self-Confidence = how you **act/ carry** yourself

| Self-Image | Self-Esteem | Self-Confidence |
|---|---|---|
| Think | Feel | Act |

Confidence is an inside job. It is your inner work that makes you stronger so you have the courage to step out and be seen. When you feel good about yourself, you are more inclined to take risks. Work on your self-image and self-esteem. Change the way you think and feel about yourself. The more established you are in thinking and feeling good about yourself, the more willing you are to act. When you act, confidence is built. Take small risks to get small wins. Small wins make you feel good setting you up to take on bigger risks. Bigger risks garner bigger rewards. If you want success, become confident. Success follows confidence.

The amount of confidence you have is directly related to how willing you are to take risks knowing you could have a loss, disappointment or setback. Be able to take a loss without getting completely defeated. One setback should not shut you down that you are unable to try again. If your foundation is shaken by one disappointment, go inward to build your strength then step out and try again.

Confidence increases when your inner work becomes a practice. Make the act of confidence building a regular practice. It is equivalent to filling up your car with gas. If you run out of gas, you must stop to refuel so you can continue on your journey. Make regular fill ups on your Inner Self so you do not run out of emotional gas on your life journey.

Fill ups:

- Remind yourself what you have to offer.
- Think of the times when you won AND when you lost and survived.
- Be self-deprecating. Be willing to laugh at yourself.
- Think of how far you have come. You have made progress in the face of setbacks and disappointment.
- Love yourself in its entirety.
- You are not alone. Everyone's path is littered with setbacks, losses and disappointments.
- You have time. Just get going with your plans.
- Develop daily practices that lift you up: prayer, mantras, notes on your mirrors. Be your best cheerleader.

Confidence is also energy. What does your energy say about you? How do you present yourself to the world? Confidence is attractive. When you let your beautiful, strong light shine bright, you spend less time searching for opportunities because opportunities find you. When you are confident, you are in alignment with your Highest Self because you know your worth. You know how beautiful and amazing you really are.

Confidence is worthiness in action.

What can you say or do to boost your confidence?

*"Desperation should not be the reason to finally show up in your life"*

## Soul R$_x$ #24

## Get Out Of Your Own Way

Many want dreams to come true, a situation to advance, a relationship to develop, or more joy, yet struggle to push forward to make it happen. Perhaps there is a strong desire emanating from inside you, but you cannot connect to the action required. So, what is holding you back? Mostly what stands between you and what you want is YOU. I often hear people say that they need to "get out of their own way." They are admittedly sick of listening to themselves. They know what they want, but are paralyzed to create movement. Some of the contributors to inaction is your mindset, your beliefs, what you think about yourself, what others will think about you or your lack of self-esteem.

Not getting out of your own way can feel painful. Find someone who knows what they want or knows who they want to be and does not live in accordance with that knowing and you will find someone in real pain. Pain looks like frustration, anger, unhappiness, or sadness. It is almost as if your Soul is pushing you out of the nest, urging you to fly. How much pain can you really take before you create the change you are seeking? You know deep down you want to grow, be, or do something different. Often the pain of remaining immobilized becomes so painful that you cannot stand it any longer and must do something to create movement toward your goal. Unfortunately, sometimes people are only willing to do something when they are forced or are desperate such as an illness or a relationship break up. Desperation should not be the reason to finally show up in your life.

Getting out of your own way requires a commitment to your Soul's longing. Step away from your Inner Critic and step into alignment with your Highest Self. Operate from that space. Ask yourself, "What am I willing to do to get out of my own way?"

To get out of your own way:

- Dial down the negative talk in your head.
- Create a list of your limiting beliefs, examine them and find which one(s) are holding you back.
- Start focusing on good self talk.
- Action! What is one thing you could do to get movement on what you want?
- Hire a Life Coach to help you get clarity and move through your fears.
- Seek professional help with a counsellor.
- Write out affirmations that speak your truth…"I am well, I am kind, I am compassionate." Give voice to a rant that makes you feel good about yourself.
- Accept where you are knowing you cannot change the road you travelled on, but you can change the road ahead.
- Find the easiest point of entry to your dream.
- Love yourself which means accept who you are and know that is enough.
- Recognize what you fear. Choose one and challenge it with action.
- Find a group to support you.
- Connect yourself NOW to the amazing feelings of achieving your future goal.
- Forgive so you can move on from the anger that may be holding you back.

What is your biggest obstacle to getting out of your own way?

*"The best way to take care of others is to take care of yourself first."*

## Soul R<sub>x</sub> #25

## *Remember Yourself*

Before an airplane takes off, the flight crew reviews the flight emergency procedures including a reminder that should the cabin pressure change, an oxygen mask will drop. You are advised to put the mask on yourself first before helping others. This is an excellent metaphor for life. The best way to take care of others is to take care of yourself first.

If you are a giver or caretaker, you can easily lose yourself in the process of caring for others. It happens so gradually that you may not even notice it. This is especially true of those who have a caregiver mindset. These are people who love to take care of others by helping in any way possible. Caregiver types can easily be overwhelmed with demands and expectations from spouses, families, friends, bosses, or co-workers who will slowly suck the energy out of them.

Remember to take care of yourself first by taking care of your:

- Health
- Energy
- Emotions
- Personal growth
- Money
- Mindset
- Relationships

Bring joy back to your life by remembering yourself. It is too important; your life depends on it. You cannot give others what you do not have. If you have your own health, you are in a better position to help someone else take care of theirs. If you have strong emotional health, you are in a better position to help others through their struggles. If you have a positive mindset, you are more likely to influence others in a positive way.

Remember yourself.

In what area of your life do you need to remember yourself?

*"Joy does not slip away from you; you slip away from joy."*

## Soul R<sub>x</sub> #26

## Be The Gatekeeper Of Your Joy

Where's my joy? Some days it felt like it was hidden. Why would I feel great one day and not the next? I love feeling joyful. Who does not want to feel good more often than not? Why can joy be so inconsistent? It felt like life was happening to me and that I had no control. I thought there must be a better way to go through life than feeling like you are riding an emotional rollercoaster. I got a taste of joy and then it disappeared. I was fed up. Joy should not be so elusive. I was tired of feeling down then up and then down again. I loved the feeling of joy so much that I made a commitment to protect it with fierce determination, but first I had to find it.

Where is consistent joy found? My search included reading spiritual books, listening to soulful podcasts, paying attention and being introspective about my life. After much Soul searching, I realized joy resides with my Highest Self. Joy shares the same space as the present moment, gratitude and appreciation. I became my own test dummy eventually realizing that joy does not slip away from me; I slip away from joy. I decided to take charge. It was as if I was riding in the passenger seat of a car and had an epiphany. I was in the wrong seat. I opened the door, slammed it shut, marched around the front of the car eyeing up the driver's seat, opened the driver's door and slipped behind the wheel. I had made a decision. I was in control of my joy. I fiercely determined that joy was no longer going to be conditional. Sad events happen, bad days occur, but there was something bigger, broader, more meaningful that was always walking with me, my Highest Self. Joy was found there. I was determined to stay in a relationship with my Highest Self.

Aligning with your Highest Self means staying connected to your joy. This is a choice. Perhaps you wonder how does one stay joyful when someone upsets you? People do not steal your joy, you walk away from it. When drama unfolds, you have practiced walking away from your joy. It is unconscious living. Staying with your joy is practiced. This is conscious living. Faltering is part of the human condition. It is how you learn. It shows you what you do not want, so you can actively show what you do want. Wanting joy is wanting to be in alignment with your Highest Self. When you falter, the speed at which you return to your joy is a sign of your spiritual maturity. Spiritual maturity is a sign you want more for yourself and your human experience.

You cannot control what happens to you, but you can control how you react to situations. When you react negatively, you move away from your joy. When a situation upsets you and you choose anything else other than peace, you walk away from your joy. Pay attention to your emotional state. Staying with your joy is a matter of attention.

What walks you from your joy?

Do you allow yourself to be pulled into drama?
Do you allow a driver cutting you off in traffic to steal your joy?
Do you spend time talking about what is wrong with the world rather than what is right with it?
Do you focus on lack in your life rather than abundance?

How does focusing on lack in your life make you feel? How does focusing on abundance make you feel? Go with the one that makes you feel good. Do not allow the behaviour of others to lure you from your joy. When you stay with your joy, you become an observer of the chaos and not a participant of it. Where do you want to put your attention? Joy is dependent on your attention.

Joy exists, but you have to stay with it. The crack in the door of joy widens with the attention that you bring to it. Well placed attention creates the experience of sustainable joy. The practice of staying with your joy is the practice of staying in alignment with your Highest Self.

Be a fierce protector of your joy.

What is one thing you can begin doing today to practice being in a state of joy?

*"Shift from self-loathing to self-loving."*

## Soul R<sub>x</sub> #27

## *Love Your Body*

Think of everything that your body is capable of doing. It is a sophisticated system of signals giving you life every day. Your heart beats, your lungs breathe, your legs take you where you want to go, your eyes see. Even if one part of your body fails, you have other avenues to experience life. It is truly amazing. Fall in love with your body.

You cannot allow the outer world to dictate your relationship with your body. You live in a world where you are bombarded by images telling you how your body should look. These external messages create wedges that separate you from your Highest Self. Marketing messages inflame the Ego which then sends messages of self loathing to your body, "I don't look like that." "I wish I looked like that." Most of the images have been perfected with digital imaging such as removing lines on faces and making body parts appear skinnier than they are. The outer world is constructing a body image that is unreasonable and unattainable. You must set a new standard for your body. Self-love is an outgoing message, not an incoming one.

To begin to change your relationship with your body, love it the way it is. Gratitude is an awesome way to appreciate yourself. Use gratitude to bestow blessings on your body. What gratitude can you express toward your body? What does your body do for you every day that you are grateful for? Gratitude directed at your body raises your level of appreciation putting you on the path of accepting yourself.

Next, switch to articulating what you love about your body. I love my eye colour. It is unique. I love the shape of my lips. I love how strong I am. I love how I walk. Showing love for your body may prove to be a very difficult task at first, but keep up the practice. You will only gain momentum if you consistently have this perspective. As you begin to point out what you love about yourself, you build a loving relationship with you. End your love rant with, "I love and accept myself."

Shift from self-loathing to self-loving. When you love yourself completely, you end the war with yourself. Loving and accepting yourself completely sets you free.

What would truly loving your body do for you?

*"Your Ego separates you from who you really are."*

## Soul R$_x$ #28

## *Break Up With Yourself*

When I became a Life Coach, conversations with others became interesting and rich because I learned to listen deeply. I soon became aware of the struggles that people often face. One of the comments I can recall hearing from many people is, "I am sick of hearing my own voice." This comment refers to the Ego's constant ticker tape of thought. I can relate to this Ego driven monologue because I had statements that looped over and over again in my head such as, "What am I going to do with my life?" I was sick of hearing my voice too. I did not know how to properly answer my question, so my Ego answered my question for me. It sounded like, "Life is so hard to figure out. I am never going to figure this out. I don't know what I am supposed to be doing with my life." None of these answers were useful to me and quite frankly perpetuated my fears around what I should be doing with my life. I should not have trusted the quality of the source. My Ego's best friend, the Inner Critic, was the storyteller.

Develop an awareness that your Ego exists. Recognize when you are living from your Ego centered self. Be alert to your Inner Critic, otherwise, you are at the mercy of the stories it tells. Breaking up with yourself is breaking up with your Ego. It is only when you break free of your Ego that you can recognize the difference between what your Ego has to offer you and what your Highest Self has to offer you. When your spiritual awareness activates, you realize you are not the voice in your head. You are so much bigger than that. Struggles originate in an Ego centered life.

Breaking up with yourself:

- allows you to create a new story, a much kinder loving story about you. Your Ego has an old storyline to which it holds tightly and likes to repeat. Breaking away from it allows the old storyline to stop. Begin storytelling from your Highest Self.

- is freedom. You become unshackled from the confines of the old stories and limiting beliefs when you choose to invest in a relationship with your Higher Self. You can allow yourself to feel good again by embracing love, by being love, by thinking good thoughts, by assuming things are working out for you. Better stories come from the place of unconditional love.

- is an exercise in spiritual maturity. When you decide that you are done with struggle, you are deciding to live less from your Ego. When you recognize you want better for yourself and are willing to explore what your Highest Self has to offer you, your life shifts.

Break the dependency on your Ego. It only serves to separate you from who you really are.

What would breaking up with your Ego do for you?

*"The giving and receiving of a compliment is a Soul to Soul transaction."*

## Soul R$_x$ #29

## *Accept The Compliment*

Acceptance of self shows up in many ways including accepting compliments. Compliments or acknowledgements are a way for others to bestow love on you. Compliments are gifts. Allow others to give you the gift of love.

There is no denying it feels good when you are paid a compliment. Compliments are fuel. They are an instant boost to your self-esteem. I remember doing writing exercises with two friends. My friend who was leading one of the exercises asked us to think of two people. Unbeknownst to them, I chose the two friends who were sitting in front of me. The next part of the exercise was to write down acknowledgements about these two individuals. When it came time to share what we had written, I declared that it was the two of them that I had chosen for the exercise. All of a sudden, my two friends were filled with excitement. They adjusted their clothing, fluffed up their hair like a couple of chickens flapping their wings and readjusted themselves in their seats as if they were about to listen to the best story ever. They *really* perked up when I revealed it was them I had chosen to write about. What this experience told me is that people love hearing about themselves. It makes them feel good. It is not every day that people dole out compliments. Take the love in and send it back out. Make more people feel good. Showering others with compliments is the easiest thing to do because it costs you nothing.

When people compliment you, they are making an authentic connection. They see you. They want you to know that. Accept it. Too often people give compliments or provide acknowledgements only to have them deflected. Sometimes the compliment exchange gets awkward. I witnessed this in action one evening as I watched an exchange between two women unfold. One woman approached the other, who she had obviously not seen in a long time. She exclaimed how wonderful she looked. The woman receiving the compliment responded with, "My hair is greasy." I have been guilty of this myself. Someone gives me a compliment only to have me downplay it or point out something that I think is not my best feature or reveal a secret about what I am not good at. The act of deflection is dishonouring yourself as well as dishonouring the other person who wants to bestow some love on you. Allow the authentic connection to happen. The giving and receiving of a compliment is a Soul to Soul transaction. It is a gift from one Highest Self to another.

Become practiced at receiving compliments. When someone acknowledges you through a compliment, believe it, accept it, and enjoy it. The words "thank you" are the simplest form of receipt.

What needs to happen for you to begin accepting compliments?

# INSPIRATION

*"Inspiration is receiving the breath of God."*

## Soul R<sub>x</sub> #30

## Create And Hold The Space For Inspiration

For years I thought about being a writer. I was always waiting on inspiration to strike like a lightning bolt or a heavenly message whispered in my ear, "This is the time to begin." I never felt inspired. It seemed inspiration was out there somewhere, but only certain people were marked for it. I have learned, however, that inspiration is accessible to everyone.

Inspiration is like electricity running through your home. The electricity in my house is already there, but if I want to use a lamp or charge my phone I must plug into the outlet. It is my job as a writer to plug into the outlet of inspiration which has always been there. When I first decided to begin writing, I easily became restless. I wiggled in my chair feeling uncomfortable in my own skin, rolling my head back and forth loosening my neck muscles as if that was the issue. Instead of popping out of my seat to avoid being uncomfortable, I eventually decided to sit in my seat for longer periods of time writing whatever came to me on the topic I had chosen. I decided to type without judging the words on the screen. At first, I wrote insignificant sentences then eventually the good stuff showed up. It was as if I had passed a test. Could I sit quietly long enough and push through the barrier of myself? Eventually I realized plugging into inspiration for me meant sitting down, getting quiet and being fully present in the moment while waiting it out like a cop on her shift sitting in her car waiting for the suspect to show up. This was the art of creating and holding the space for inspiration. With patience and presence, I signaled inspiration to be released allowing it to flow through me.

I accept there is a greater force guiding me. When I connect to inspiration, I am in union with my Highest Self. The word inspiration means "to communicate to the spirit." The Bible is considered to be inspired by God or God-breathed. Inspiration, then, is receiving the breath of God. Open yourself up to allow inspiration to flow through you.

Whether you are an entrepreneur, a stay at home mom, a manager, a student, allow yourself to be inspired by creating and holding the space of inspiration. Imagine what would happen if you plugged into the outlet of inspiration. Imagine what amazing ideas would be breathed into you.

How can you create and hold the space for inspiration?

*"Authenticity is originality."*

## Soul R$_x$ #31

## *Be The Inspiration*

We tend to lean on other's stories for inspiration. Being inspired or consuming other's lives is easy. In a heavily connected world, thanks to social media, we are bombarded by images and stories of people living their best lives.

It is inspiring, exciting and fun to watch people climb to the top of their game. If you are always consuming other's lives, however, the message that you send yourself is success, dreams, attempts, desires, wishes fulfilled are for other people. Make the shift from needing inspiration to being the inspiration.

The best way to be an inspiration is to show up authentically as you to live out the life you want. People connect with authenticity and authenticity is originality. Living out your dreams inspires others. Listen to your inner voice that is constantly whispering messages of desires, dreams, and callings and have the courage to live in accordance with it. People are inspired by that kind of boldness.

Life wants your originality. Be the inspiration.

What could you start doing to be the inspiration?

*"Leave people better than you found them."*

## Soul R$_x$ #32

## *Be An Encourager*

One of the easiest ways to help yourself is to help others. The simplest form of help is encouragement. It costs you nothing, but pays big dividends to both the receiver and the sender. A few years ago, a friend and I were working toward health goals. We would text each other our weight loss achievements. When she sent me a text, I would always send her a return text complimenting her on a job well done. If she felt discouraged, I'd just send a simple note saying "keep going, you got this." It was just a quick note of encouragement. Nothing major. I never thought anything of it.

About a year later, my friend was setting more health goals. She texted me asking me if she could send me her weigh in number each week. She told me the encouraging feedback she received from me the previous year helped her and made her feel good. I thought, "Really?" I did not even realize sending a few words of encouragement to her had an impact. I have received similar feedback from others too. "Wow, I feel great after talking to you." I remind others of their awesomeness with a few simple words. You never know how you are impacting people. Something insignificant to you might be impactful to someone else. To compliment and praise someone might be the turnaround point in their day. Make it your philosophy to leave people better than you found them. Encouragement is a way to do that.

Take encouragement to the next level by acknowledging someone versus just complimenting them. Point out how someone shows up in life. An acknowledgement speaks to the person's qualities. It is very powerful because it speaks to a person's being-ness.

Examples of acknowledgement are:

"You really demonstrated how much you cared when you took the extra few minutes to help your co-worker."
Quality demonstrated: caring

"The excellence that you deliver in your work inspires other people to do their best."
Quality demonstrated: excellence

"It is evident that you possess an entrepreneurial approach to your work."
Quality demonstrated: entrepreneurial spirit

"Travelling hours to visit your ill friend really shows how much you appreciate friendship."
Quality demonstrated: kindness

"You are really great at designing a quilt."
Quality demonstrated: creativity

Acknowledgement as a form of encouragement says, "I see you. I see who you really are as a person." Articulating qualities is powerful because most people just want to be seen. Encouragement makes a difference in the world as it is the same as throwing a pebble into a lake. There is a ripple effect. One will never know how a simple uplifting statement will shift someone on their path.

The world needs more encouragers.

Who needs your encouragement?

*"Wonder connects you with your Soul."*

# Soul R_x #33

# *Dance With Wonder*

Everyone has dreams. Some are small dreams giving you nervous butterflies. Some dreams are so large they scare you. All dreams start with wonder. Wonder is how your Highest Self nudges you toward your dreams. Wonder connects you with your Soul.

"I" and "wonder" are two words that become magical when combined. Long before I attempted to write this book, I would wonder what was possible for me.

I wonder if I commit to writing a book, could I do it?
I wonder if I start writing, would anything show up on the page?
I wonder if I became a motivational speaker, what message would I deliver?
I wonder if I commit to being a speaker and author, how would my life change?

It turns out I could commit to writing a book. I found that when I committed to writing on a regular basis, the words I wanted showed up on the page. I began to trust the writing process. Through the writing process, I found the message I wanted to deliver to the world. I wrote my way out of challenging ideas. I have already given one motivational speech based on the teachings of this book. I have never felt more aligned with my purpose. I cannot wait to find out how else my life will change as the result of producing this book. Dancing with wonder has helped me to live a more fulfilled life and to live a life on purpose.

Build your own wonder statements. Creating them builds excitement and helps you create a vision for your goals. Have you ever wondered what is possible for your life? Ask yourself big questions. You will find your big answers. Questions allow you to dance with wonder.

I wonder if…..

….I changed who I spend time with, how would my life change?
….I stopped complaining and starting expressing gratitude, what shift would I notice?
….I explored starting my own business, would I really do it?
….I pushed myself outside my comfort zone, what would I achieve?
….I set a goal so large it scared me, how much could I achieve?
….I trained for a marathon, could I run the entire race?

Wonder is the catalyst to your dreams. Let your wonder guide you to living a truly incredible life.

What do you wonder about?

*"Positive energy is attractive."*

## Soul R$_x$ #34

## *Be An Influential Energy Source*

Energy matters. Often energy gets described as a "vibe" or "feeling." "I am not getting a good vibe about that person," or "I just feel like the person is so genuine." Energy is an invisible force that you tap into to give you information. Have you ever had an experience where a particular person enters the room and the energy drops. "Who brought the buzz kill?" The opposite is also true. If someone is displaying high energy and walks into a room, the energy in the room raises to meet it. Energy, therefore, is a powerful source. Positive energy trumps negative energy.

Do you want to be a powerful person of influence in this life? Be the person emitting good vibes. Be a positive, uplifting energy wherever you go. It is needed. Dedicating time to work on raising your energy level to be a vibrant, positive force in the world is worthy work. Like a stone thrown into a pond, the ripple you create will have a compounding effect.

To raise your energy level:

- Workout. People who feel good about themselves tend to have a better attitude.
- Appreciate everything about life. Your perspective matters.
- Eat well. Choosing quality, healthy food brings you alive supplying you energy.
- Speak well of yourself and others. Words have power. Choose them wisely.

- Think good thoughts. It is hard to emit high energy if you are thinking low quality thoughts.
- Be kind. Kindness has a reciprocal effect. It makes the receiver and the giver feel good.
- Listen to uplifting music. High energy music can boost your mood.
- Read inspirational stories. Be inspired by others so you can be the inspiration.

Positive energy is attractive. I know a child who is a bright, smiling, bundle of energy. He is so positive and happy. He emits an energy that is mesmerizing. I remember taking him to the movies where he decided to play some games in the arcade before the show. Playing the games allow you to earn tickets which are redeemed to purchase small toys. On this particular day, he was short tickets for the item he wanted to purchase. He voiced what he was hoping to buy to the arcade worker, as he stood on his tippy toes with his bright eyes twinkling just above the glass counter, while flashing his large toothy smile. The game store operator gave him what he wanted. It was not a surprise to me. His energy is irresistible. When I told his parents this story, I joked that he seemed to have a strategically placed horseshoe. They both exclaimed at the same time, "We say that all the time about him!" He emits an energy that makes him easy to be around. He is easily included and treated well. It is not an accident that he gets what he wants.

Energy ebbs and flows. You are more inclined to get what you want out of life when you are a happy, positive person. Energy is powerful. It has the power to lift people up or drag them down. Be a positive, influential energy source.

What is something you can do today to raise your energy level to be an outstanding influential source?

*"All ideas first lie in the imagination waiting for you to give them life."*

## Soul R<sub>x</sub> #35

## Make Mental Movies

Imagination is the beginning of reality. As a young child, I watched a show called Mr. Dressup, which led the young viewing audience through songs, stories, and crafts. In one of the segments, Mr. Dressup sat at his tilted drawing board with a large sheet of white paper. He started with his pencil and an idea, then he would begin to draw. He would look into the camera challenging the kids who were watching to use their imagination, "What should we add next?" Through the lens of the camera, kids like me watched as, stroke by stroke, he brought a scene to life to tell a story. He slowly drew additional details and colour. What began as an idea quickly developed into a vivid picture.

All ideas first lie in the imagination waiting for you to give them life. You have the capability to bring dreams to life just like Mr. Dressup brought stories to life on paper. Start by imagining that you are the artist. What is lying in your imagination? Write down, draw, or find pictures of your big ideas first, in the category you are hoping to make progress. Is the category business? Finances? Spirituality? Career? Slowly add details, but be bold. Dream in colour. Really fill in the specifics after you establish the general area on which you want to focus.

For example, are you looking for a career change? Imagine the drawing board. Begin with the category that is calling you to expand. Are you working in a job that is alright for now, but you know you have bigger dreams. What do you imagine for yourself? A teacher? Imagine you have your colouring pencil. Begin filling in the details. Who do you see yourself teaching? Is there an age group? Are you a kindergarten teacher or a University Professor? What do you want to teach? What excites you about being a teacher? This is not the time to entertain your Inner Critic, the negative voice that tells you why it cannot be done. This is a time to devote yourself to your imagination. What do you want?

The dream details are important to help define your vision and ignite your excitement about embarking on a new journey. Your dream can come true. Do not abandon it before it is given life. Give your dream a chance. Feel how amazing it would be to accomplish it. Imagine what your life would look like once you are a teacher. Imagine yourself earning more money, being creative, having your own classroom, being a mentor to others. Get in touch with the emotional side of accomplishing your dream.

Once you activate your imagination and excitement, move your dream along. Answer this question: What is something you could execute in the next 24 hours to move yourself closer to your dream? Is it talking to someone who is a teacher? Perhaps find yourself a mentor who can help you with your journey. Is it identifying the requirements to become a teacher? Action moves you toward your dream becoming a reality. Allow yourself the luxury of dreaming big and bold and in detail. Your ideal life is waiting to jump off the page and into reality.

What mental movie do you want to create?

*"You do not need perfection, you need a starting point."*

## Soul R<sub>x</sub> #36

## Create A Starting Point For Your Dreams

A few years ago, I enrolled in a John Maxwell leadership program. The man that leads the program is named Paul Martinelli. Paul has a very interesting and inspiring story. He came from a family of successful, educated siblings, but felt like he did not measure up because he stuttered. Believing he was not as smart as the rest of his family or anyone else around him, he dropped out of school and worked in dead end jobs. His last job was a roofer which was back breaking work. Eventually Paul decided he wanted more out of life for himself, so he started a cleaning business.

His business began when he grabbed a bucket of water, a scrubbing brush and a squeegee. He walked down to a corner in town and started washing the windows of a business. As all businesses do, they have gate keepers. The gate keeper comes running out shouting, "Hey, we didn't hire you to wash our windows." Paul would say, "True. But how are you going to know how well I will clean the rest of your office if you don't know how well I clean your windows." This was his icebreaker to get clients although he had no clue how to build a business. He did not let his lack of knowledge in building a business stop him either. One of Paul's great sayings is, "Build your wings on the way down." His starting point was a leap.

Paul's boldness is inspiring. Like Paul, sometimes you have to be pushed to your limit before you decide you want something different for yourself. What is beautiful about Paul's story is how he began his new dream. Too often you wait for something to be perfect, to have all the knowledge or wait to be validated, when all you really need is a starting point. Paul kick-started his dreams by grabbing his bucket of water and heading to the first street corner that had a business. You do not need perfection, you need a starting point.

Excuses move your starting point. Stop making excuses and find a reason to start. Are you tired of where you are in your life? Need extra money? Want to feel fulfilled? Want to feel purposeful? Want to see how far you can really go in life? If Paul could start with a bucket of water, what is the smallest thing you could start with?

What can you use as a starting point for your dream?

*"Me too, are comforting words to hear."*

## Soul R$_x$ #37

## *You Are Not Alone*

There is comfort in numbers. When you experience inner turmoil, it often feels like you are the only one going through it. One benefit that comes with age is the realization that you share common aspirations, dreams, concerns, and struggles with others. There are others wanting the same goals as you. There are people who are scared like you. There are people who have big dreams just like you.

Recall a time when you have been sitting in an audience where the speaker asks if there are any questions. Perhaps you had a question in mind, but thought it might be a stupid or irrelevant one to ask, then someone else raises their hand with the exact same question. The person who had the courage to ask validates you. It was not a stupid question to ask. Over time an awakening begins to happen. You realize there are many people thinking and feeling the same way as you whether it is something simple like asking a question or something more significant like being unsure of what to do in life.

Sharing your feelings, desires, dreams, frustrations, and concerns has two advantages:

- It gets reflected back to you that you are not alone
- You show others that they are not alone.

Common concerns unite Souls. *Me too* are comforting words to hear. There is relief in knowing you are not alone.

With whom can you share your aspirations and concerns?

*"Enthusiasm is contagious."*

## Soul R$_x$ #38

## Be Enthusiastic

If you are enthusiastic others will be too. Enthusiasm is contagious. When you offer up enthusiasm to the world, it responds with enthusiasm. It is a high, fast flowing energy that resonates with others.

A few years ago, I remember shopping for fabric. All of a sudden, I noticed a bolt of fabric in a bin that I had been searching for. I got excited about it, exclaimed to my husband that I had finally found it and it was on sale! Suddenly, a woman walking nearby who heard my excitement, slowed down and started to circle the bin like a vulture. She was lured by my excitement. If I was excited about something then maybe she would be too. I could tell she did not want to miss out on this amazing opportunity. After a quick peek, she realized there was nothing of interest for her. She added a quick glance of judgment toward me wondering why I was so excited over burgundy and green plaid fabric with roosters. I often get accused of creating excitement. This is a small example of how enthusiasm is contagious. If you are excited, other people will be too.

People want to be energized because it is a wonderful feeling. People follow high energy because it is easy, it is powerful AND people are changed by it. How can you get more enthusiasm in your life? Easy. Choose to be enthusiastic; it is a choice. Start with one thing that is going well then begin appreciating what else is going well. Notice how your energy changes, the momentum shifts and picks up speed. Try being enthusiastic, for example, if you have a job you like, but do not love, create enthusiasm by expressing appreciation..."I have a job.

Many others are out of work. I can support myself with this job. It provides money to feed my family and put a roof over our heads. I have met really interesting people at my workplace. I have many friends here. I have opportunity to grow here. I have a boss that I really like working for. She lets me be flexible with my schedule when I have to be. Not everyone has that kind of flexibility. I know I don't have to stay in this job forever. I can choose something else. There are certain parts of my job that I like a lot. (Name them.) I work for a company that is growing. I am excited to be a part of a dynamic team."

Momentum can easily get shifted by focusing on appreciation and gratitude. Enthusiasm is born out of this space. Practice being enthusiastic. Feel the shift within you.

What can you get excited about in your life?

*"There is always more to come for you."*

## Soul R$_x$ #39

## *Be A Living Work of Art*

You are a masterpiece in motion. You are an example of continuous unfolding - a living, breathing work of art. Live life like a gorgeous piece of artwork. Would people be in awe of your life? As a life maker, you are in constant creation. You get to add richness and depth to your story. As long as you are living, you get to change, add, and sculpt your story. Be the master artist of your own life. Your life is an exquisite moving piece of art. Bring it to life with your uniqueness. Even when you have chosen wrong or faltered or did not show up as your best self today, you have the opportunity to work on your masterpiece. Do not give up on your beautiful life.

Exercise: Create a real life art series.

Your life could be viewed as a series of paintings each one telling a story of each segment of your life. As a fun exercise, break your life into several segments (into three equal parts, or by decade or by themes such as teen years, university, marriage). Paint works of art to reflect your life during each of those times. You do not need to use a canvas and paints. Instead use 8" x 11" sheets of paper and pencil crayons or markers. What are the most important ideas you want to convey? Are you called to use bright colours? What images are you inclined to paint? What story does your artwork tell about the various stages of your life?

A painter has to determine when the last stroke of the brush is the final one. A filmmaker decides when the last scene is filmed. A songwriter finds a point when the words are arranged for the last time. As a life artist, you can continue to develop the masterpiece. You can redo, reset, or change direction. You have a beautiful life. Live it like a masterpiece. There is always more to come for you.

What story does your beautiful life tell?

*"The less baggage you carry, the more you will be at peace."*

## Soul R_x #40

## *Free Up Mental Space*

When I began working in the corporate world, computers were less sophisticated than they are now. Hard drives were not large. Every time a file was deleted, it actually got broken into bits and distributed over your hard drive eventually causing your computer to run less effectively. Once your computer started operating slowly, it was time to do a d-frag. This is technical speak for cleaning up your hard drive. Running a d-frag was like taking the vacuum cleaner to your hard drive collecting all the bits to free up space so it could operate more effectively.

Sometimes you need to run a d-frag on your life. Clear up the list of to do's which are scattered across your life such as:

- Attend to the junk drawer you have been meaning to clean out.
- Organize the closet that has been nagging at you.
- Make the phone calls that need to be made.
- File the papers that are stacking up.
- Have the conversation you know you need to have.

The to-do's occupy too much mental real estate. I once heard someone say that there are people who want to save the world, but cannot find a pencil. So true. Minor activities that need attention make a lot of noise distracting you from achieving your big goals. Is it possible that the clutter under your bed is making you sleep deprived or that the stack of papers that need filing is keeping you from reaching out to new prospects in your business? If you are splitting your focus, you are not providing your undivided attention to those goals that are going to bring you the greatest return.

Perhaps the greatest return you will receive by freeing up mental clutter is creating a relationship with your Highest Self. It is difficult to be in union with that Essence when you have a noisy inner world. The less baggage you carry, the more you will be at peace. Freeing up your mental space returns you to calm and quiet allowing for focus and connection with yourself.

What list of decisions do you need to clean up to free up mental space?

*"Dreams have a price tag."*

## Soul R$_x$ #41

## *Own Your Dreams*

Within you are dreams...big dreams, small dreams, wishes, desires. Dreams are inspired; it is your Highest Self giving you ideas of how to express yourself. Have an idea that you continuously toss around in your head? Where is it coming from? Why will it not leave you? An inspired idea that will not leave you alone is like a blinking light on an answering machine reminding you that there is something waiting for you. Will you pick up the message?

To turn your inspiration into reality, take ownership of it. Growing up my dad was a mill worker and my mom was a homemaker. We lived on a modest income, so when my parents bought something, they took care of it. I remember our very first brand new car. It was a 1981 two door Black Pontiac Parisienne. We were not allowed to eat in the car. We were not allowed to drink in the car and there were towels placed on the front seats to keep the fabric from wearing out. It was washed and waxed regularly and parked only in carefully chosen parking spots. There was no mistake. My parents owned the car. When you rent cars, however, do you really care where you park it? You eat sandwiches in the rental car like you were placing a tree limb into a wood chipper. Crumbs fly everywhere. You care more when you own something. It is easy to rent a car, but to buy a car requires much more of you. Your dreams are like that.

Truly owning your dreams requires a greater investment. It often requires money, time and/or sweat equity. Dreams have a price tag. If you want them to happen, it is fully on you to make it happen. You can ask for help. Others may come on the journey with you, but the dream is yours to execute from beginning to end. Your Highest Self may have started the inspiration, but you have to finish it.

What dreams have you been longing to own?

# CONNECTION

*"Connection to your Highest Self is a two way street."*

## Soul R$_x$ #42

### Separate Your Godly Messages From Your Egoic Messages

Connection to your Highest Self is a two way street. There is a stream of consciousness that ebbs and flows between your physical self and your Highest Self. You know when you are talking to God, but it can be much more difficult to distinguish when God is talking to you because there is a mixture of thoughts streaming from two sources: your Highest Self and your Ego. Thinking is the medium through which you receive messages from your Highest Self. It is also the communication medium used by the Ego. The Ego is like that one person that you know who is always interrupting and talking over you. Thinking becomes the pipeline that funnels the collection of ideas and thoughts that your Ego manufactures and merges them with the Godly messages from your Highest Self. The garbage gets mixed with the goodness.

The onus is on you to determine from which source these thoughts originate. Develop a relationship with your Highest Self by bringing awareness to the quiet space within you so that you can decipher the Godly thoughts from those that are Egoic. Hint: The negative ones are from the Ego. They are the ones that hold you back, make you question yourself, fabricate and tell stories about situations.

One of the most effective ways that I have learned to separate the garbage from the goodness is by journaling in the mornings. I allow myself to write whatever comes to mind to get the stream of consciousness flowing. At first, I can hear the Ego streaming its usual garbage. It is best to give it space to say what it needs to say, but then something magical happens. Eventually the goodness shows up streamed from my Highest Self. On the page appears all my dreams, great ideas, inspirations, and aspirations. Sometimes a beautiful sentence appears on the page that I keep for future use. There is a lot of sludge that gets mixed in with the nuggets that are waiting for me. It is my job to decipher which is which.

The beautiful act of writing is an act of faith. Faith is believing something good is waiting for me whether it is on the page or in life. When I discovered writing was a way for me to connect with my Highest Self, I got excited to get out of bed to write each morning to hear what it had to say. I discovered that when I wrote to my Highest Self, my Highest Self wrote back. Have faith that there are beautiful messages waiting for you. Your job is to find an avenue to access those messages.

Raise your awareness to recognize which thoughts are your Godly ones and which ones are your Egoic ones.

What are ways you can communicate with your Highest Self?

*"How you feel ultimately determines what you do."*

## Soul R$_x$ #43

## Check In With Yourself

"How's your head space, man?" This is a question my friend's dad often asks her when he greets her. He is a hippie musician who gets the importance of checking on your emotional barometer. A regular check on how you are doing is a great practice that pays you huge spiritual dividends. Seeking to feel good emotionally and never assessing it would be equivalent to wanting to lose weight without ever stepping on a scale to measure how you are doing. You can only manage what you measure. Using a simple scale of 0-10 is a quick and easy measurement to identify how good you feel.

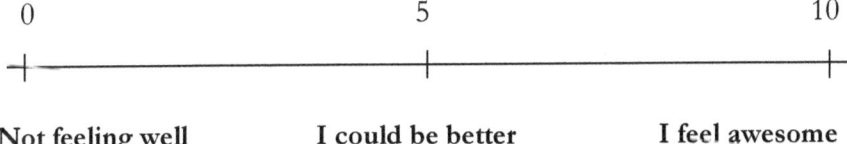

**Not feeling well**      **I could be better**      **I feel awesome**

You need to be aware of your mindset before you can do something about it. Do you need an adjustment? Regularly assessing how you are doing emotionally is important as emotion is the engine of your life. How you feel ultimately determines what you do.

How is your thinking process? How are you feeling? Ensuring you are carrying a good mindset through the day matters. Emotions create momentum. If you begin to feel badly, it seems everything wrong begins to happen, but the opposite is also true. A good mindset triggers good things to happen in your life. Unless you recalibrate your thinking from time to time, your resident Inner Critic who lives in your head rent free will keep you from your amazing life.

Take an emotional inventory assessment:

- Do I feel good?
- What leftover residue am I carrying forward from the past?
- Are the words I am using positive or negative?
- What's my attitude? It is a reflection of my inner state.

Take time daily to review how you are doing. Recalibrate as needed.

How is your head space right now?

*"Nature has powerful messages for you
if you pay attention to its teachings."*

## Soul R<sub>x</sub> #44

## *Allow Nature To Teach You*

You are in nature and nature is in you. Immerse yourself in nature to feel the pulse of the Universe beating within you. Feel the aliveness as you walk through a forest or stand before an ocean.

Nature is taken for granted as a beautiful backdrop to everyday life, but what is its purpose? Its stoic presence reminds you how to be. It is your greatest teacher, God's representative on Earth, demonstrating the beauty and potential of life. Listen to the secrets nature whispers. It possesses powerful messages, if you pay attention to its teachings:

- Life multiplies and expands like perennial flowers.
- Not one single wave of the ocean can stand alone without the others.
- The trees live in harmony with one another.
- Just because you cannot see the sun some days does not mean it is not there. There is always light behind the darkness.
- Life is colourful.
- The frog is not worried about what the squirrel is up to.
- Seasons arrive on time.
- Plants continue to grow as long as they can use their resources.
- It is much easier to follow the current than to paddle against it.
- Difference and variety is beautiful.
- Unusualness is captivating.

Nature has already painted the masterpiece of how to be. Life is a wonderful, expansive place of possibility where all can live in harmony while each maintaining their uniqueness. Allow yourself to be influenced by the beauty of nature.

What can nature teach you?

*"You cheat yourself of meaningful connection with others when you stop paying attention."*

## Soul R$_x$ #45

## *Listen With Purpose*

The world is much noisier today than when I was a kid. Growing up I had three channels and one of them was snowy most of the time. Now you have TV channels on every topic. You have many social media platforms on which to connect. This constant connection is all made easier with your mobile devices. Interruptions, distractions, and notifications are the norm. People and companies are competing for your attention. To prevent getting overwhelmed and distracted by the noisy world, listening with purpose helps you cut through the noise to what matters. Listening with purpose involves what you listen to and how you listen.

Choose purposefully what you listen to. Be responsible for what is streaming into your consciousness. I often went to bed listening to the news allowing it to shut off long after I was asleep. Eventually I came to the conclusion that I wanted to control what I listened to, no longer wanting to end my day with negativity whether I was awake or not. Even riding in the car, I choose to listen to uplifting music or something educational. What you listen to matters. Incoming messages affect your mood and plays with your emotions which are the engines of action. How good you feel is directly related to the likelihood of you acting on your dreams and desires. Protect your listening bubble with determination.

How do you listen? Deeply. Listening is a very powerful, practiced skill that requires full attention and awareness. Activating deep listening with others means you are focused on what the other person is saying.

You are not listening for the opportunity to respond. Practice being fully present with no distractions which means putting down the smartphone. Sometimes when I am on the telephone with my Dad, he can tell when I am checking my cell phone because I answer with dull yeses and uh-hmms and I ask him to repeat himself often. He calls me out telling me "to put down the pocket machine" (his words for a smartphone). You must make the choice to give others your undivided attention. You cheat yourself of meaningful connection with others when you stop paying attention.

Remember to activate deep listening with yourself too. Purposefully connect you with your Inner Being. Deep listening is a pathway to authentic connection with your Highest Self. Get quiet and reduce the mind chatter, not judging or editing what arises. Stillness has become a luxury; give yourself the space to be still and listen. Your Inner Being has something to say. Answers are found in the stillness.

When do you get derailed as a listener for others and for yourself?

*"Conversations matter when you are building a life of significance."*

## Soul R$_x$ #46

## *Have Meaningful Conversations*

Meaningful conversations create meaningful connections. Connection is the oxygen of life. Spend less time engaging in conversations where people are talked about and discussing things over which you have no control. Spend more time on conversations that matter.

I had an eighty year old neighbour, Jim, that I would often chat with when we were both outside doing yard work. He was a wonderful person who had interesting stories to share. After he passed away, I wished I had spent more time connecting with him as he had so much wisdom to offer. Jim had travelled all over the world. Sometimes he would leave me in awe of his stories. He often talked about what he was reading. Jim told me that he realized there was not enough time to learn everything he wanted. He wished he had spent more time reading earlier in his life. I learned from him that aging magnifies what is important. Aging creates a focus on meaning and significance. He made me think about using my time wisely in this life. I always appreciated the engaging conversations we had even though there was a forty year age gap. Meaningful conversations can truly be found everywhere.

Make conversations count. Meaningful is not synonymous with serious. Have the conversation that brings you laughter, deepens relationships, is helpful, provides insight, asks for help, inspires or leaves people better than you left them. Conversations matter when you are building a life of significance. A meaningful conversation is a Soul to Soul connection.

How can you use conversations to create more meaning and significance in your life?

*"Breathing is a lullaby for your Ego and a song for your Soul."*

## Soul R<sub>x</sub> #47

## *Use The Power of Your Breath*

The world is noisy. Companies, employers, friends, family, and marketers vie for your attention. Noise comes to you through many channels. Sometimes you just need a break. Even a small break from the attention splitting energy has benefit. Without having to book a vacation or leave the office, you can drop away from demands momentarily by understanding the power of your breath. Breathing is a basic, beautiful act that is taken for granted. Breathing is powerful as it joins you to the present moment and leads you to your Highest Self. Breathing is a lullaby for your Ego and a song for your Soul. Breathing lulls the Ego to sleep long enough for you to come in union with your Highest Self.

Use your breath to:

- lead you to a time out from chaos. Your breath transports you to quiet.
- calm you down. Close your eyes. Breathe deeply and focus on the rhythm of your breath.
- slow your thoughts. Focusing on your breathing takes you away from your thoughts.
- bring you to the present moment. This shifts your focus. Paying attention to your breath shifts you from what you are doing or thinking.
- reset a moment. It is easy to get caught up in thoughts that make you anxious. Your breath gives you the advantage of restarting with better thoughts.

It is comforting to know that there is power in getting quiet. You are not lost, just disconnected. If you feel the external world is not providing you the happiness you have sought, shift toward your Inner Being for answers. When you are pushed to the brink having nowhere to turn for help, turn inward to your Highest Self, who has been walking with you all along. You are only moments away from receiving answers that are custom to you. Your breath is the medium that transports you there.

Meditation has become popular. It is easy to see why. Meditation provides a respite from the Ego. Meditation is the progressive quieting of the mind taking you to your Highest Self. Your breath plays a key role in transporting you there. Even a meditation for a small amount of time has value. The practice of getting quiet, closing your eyes, and focusing on your breath so that the thoughts begin to slow or stop, allows your mind to rest and offers the benefit of refreshment.

Consider giving yourself the gift of the present moment when the noise of life becomes overwhelming. Remember the power of your breath.

How would even small amounts of quiet time benefit you?

*"When you achieve authentic connection, you are acknowledging the Highest Self in another."*

## Soul R<sub>x</sub> #48

## *Seek A Circle of Like Minded People*

Surrounding yourself with like minded people is not about being with those who think the same as you or tell you what you want to hear. It is about being with people who share common interests or values.

- If you want to grow, be peaceful, be positive, and imagine amazing possibilities, find people who value that.
- If you want to grow as a leader, find people who value learning about leadership.
- If you want to learn how to be an entrepreneur, find people and groups that are interested in pursuing this avenue.
- If you want to be more spiritual, find groups that appreciate spiritual growth.

When you seek like minded people with whom you share similar interests and values, you achieve authentic connections. You know it. It feels like you are home when you meet the right people. Authentic connections allow you to build a community of people who support you. When you are supported, you do not feel alone. When you do not feel alone, you are more likely to be open to learning and sharing.

It is the diversity within the group of like minded people that allows you to increase. Other's perspectives, beliefs, knowledge, and ideas rub up against your ideas to sharpen your awareness, refine your abilities or challenge your beliefs so you can expand fully into your pursuits. Creating a like minded circle is not about quantity; it is about quality.

When you achieve authentic connection, you are acknowledging the Highest Self in another. The authentic connection gives you the permission to let your guard down so that you can be real and challenged without judgement. It is the ability for you to be raw and real which enables you to grow.

What would surrounding yourself with a like minded group do for you?

*"To reclaim your quiet space is to keep connection with your Highest Self."*

## Soul R$_x$ #49

## *Reclaim Time For Personal Connection*

One of the greatest detachments from your Highest Self is the constant bombardment of distractions from the outside world. Unless boundaries are set, your peace is constantly disrupted with rings, dings and notifications. When I was a child, there were fewer technology distractions. The telephone and television were the only disruptors. My father would be amazed at how people knew it was supper time. He would complain that as soon as we sat down to eat supper, the phone rang. We were not allowed to answer it. I also remember sitting at the table as a teenager propping myself up on my knees to peek past my father into the living room hoping to get a glimpse of a scene from General Hospital. Luke and Laura were not welcome in our home for dinner. My father would always get up from the kitchen table, march into the living room and slam the button to off. He did not like all the chaos during supper time. There were no exceptions.

In today's world your mobile devices provide a steady stream of distractions. The technology that allows you to be efficient, productive, and connected also allows you to be inefficient, unproductive and disconnected. It is up to you to place controls on interruptions. You cannot renew your relationship with your Inner Self in a noisy world.

Recently we got a new cell phone plan for our family. Three phones with 2G of data. I soon realized how much data gets used by three people checking phones incessantly when we are outside our home. I was not going to spend more money on data plans. I made a request to my teenagers to turn off data disabling the ability to post pictures to social media or download music outside our home. I decided to shut off my data too. What I soon realized is that I gained back a little sanity. While waiting for children in the car after school or shopping at the mall, waiting in the doctor's office, or waiting in line, I no longer mindlessly checked apps, updates and emails. I began using the time to reflect, meditate, get a little mind rest by sitting in silence or staying focused on tasks. Instead of incessantly checking my phone, I took the time to purposefully connect with myself. Checking mobile devices often, become addictions constantly interrupting your sanity.

Carve out time to connect with your Highest Self. It is the greatest relationship you will have. It is a divine connection where you will find peace, comfort, joy, and confidence. Put boundaries around your peace. To reclaim your quiet space is to maintain your connection with your Inner Self. It is important that you teach your children how to do this too. When you lead by example, your children learn that this connection is sacred.

How can you regain small amounts of time to keep connection with yourself?

*"You take the spiritual high road not to be THE better person,
but to be A better person."*

## Soul R$_x$ #50

## *Take The Spiritual High Road*

Life is not without adversity. Although it may not be obvious in the moment, it is through contrast that you grow. Conflicts are great teaching grounds reflecting back to you:

- what you want
- what you do not want
- with whom you want to spend your time
- what you will tolerate
- where your boundaries are
- what your limiting beliefs are
- what situations challenge you
- how you deal with conflict

Adversity forces you to be a better version of yourself. Getting through life without some adversity is impossible, but when you face challenges, do not lose yourself in the difficulty. Conflicts are for learning, but they should not steal your peace. When you are presented with a difficult situation, it is best to take the spiritual high road. You take the spiritual high road not to be *the* better person, but to be *a* better person. The high road is for you. Indicating you are going to be *the* better person in a situation is an Ego play essentially saying, "I am better than you. I know how to behave better." This attitude will not grow you. When you choose to be *a* better person, you are making a personal commitment to operate from your Highest Self. You are choosing to be a better version of you. That is something to be proud of.

When you choose to react to a difficult situation from a place of peace, you honour the spiritual connection with yourself. You are choosing not to walk away from your joy, peace, clarity, or mindfulness. Your intention in the midst of conflict is not to suffer or to cause additional suffering even if the situation is created by the other person. You can walk away from a difficult situation knowing you exited it better than you entered it. You can walk away feeling good about how you handled yourself. That is the high road.

When you decide how you want to show up in this world, back it up with action. Bring yourself in alignment with your Highest Self to strengthen your spiritual connection.

What has adversity taught you?

*"You cannot control what goes on around you,
but you can control what goes on within you."*

## Soul R<sub>x</sub> #51

## *Protect Your Peace*

Peace is power because you can control whether you have it or not. It is what everybody wants including every beauty pageant contestant. Before you have peace in your relationships, your family and in the world, you must first have personal peace. Wanting peace is noble, but choosing to live in peace is admirable.

As I write this chapter, my mother is not well. I pray for a miracle. I hope I can rewrite this chapter, but I am not fooled by her slow decline. I want this to be different for her, for me, for my father, for my family, but I do not have control over it. I have tried to control it only to find myself sad, powerless and physically manifesting symptoms that were hurting me. Over the past five years, I have watched the slow decline of my mother. From this experience, I have learned my spiritual practice is to stay in peace regardless of the circumstances. Things do not have to be working out for me in order for me to experience peace. On the outside, it appears like the situation is not working out. It is not what I want or what my family wants, but I have learned to surrender to what it is and not to mentally exhaust myself with the situation. Sometimes I falter and start fighting against it again with one last desperate attempt to help, but then I gain awareness and return to peace. I have done everything in my power to help the situation. The best thing I can do is to help myself be well, so that I can help others and be present for my mother.

Calm is found in the eye of a hurricane. Raging winds rotate around the eye. Life can be like a storm. Practice keeping yourself in the eye of the storm. That is where the most peace is found. You cannot control what goes on around you, but you can control what goes on within you. Peace is a daily choice. When you choose peace, you are willing to detach yourself from the emotional storm of external circumstances.

Having peace is separate from:

- having to be right.
- things working out for you.
- conflict. You can engage in difficult situations without losing your peace.
- other people's opinions and judgements of you.

Having peace is a place from which you navigate life's challenges rather than leaving your peace behind to deal with life's challenges. Life will always swirl around you like a storm. In a weak moment, you can falter, getting involved in the drama of life, but you always have a beautiful choice. You can walk back to peace, but in order to do that you must value it. You must value your peace more than the drama of life.

As you begin your day, be mindful to practice peace. This may have to be a moment to moment practice until you get good at it.

Strategies for peace:

- Breathe.
- Have a mantra that settles you into peace such as "I am well." "Be calm." "I'm OK."
- Be aware of your daily triggers before you even reach the point of spinning out of control.
- Create such a strong desire for peace that you will accept nothing less.

- Know you have a choice.

Peace leads you to joy, inspiration, and creativity because it is the Soul's language. When you connect with peace, you connect with your Highest Self.

How would choosing peace help you?

*"Listen and know the answers will come."*

## Soul R<sub>x</sub> #52

## *Listen To The Longing*

Longing is a nudge from your Highest Self asking you to pay attention. Perhaps there is a feeling inside that you want to do something else with your life or you feel like you need to make a change or there is a sense of wanting more fulfillment and meaning in your life. Knowing how to interpret the longing can feel confusing, so ignoring it feels like a good option. Turning away from the voice within, however, is placing distance between you and your Highest Self. Turning away is only temporary as the longing will always be in the background bubbling up from time to time until it gets addressed.

Listening acknowledges the longing. Listening is stepping into your Highest Self to hear what it has to say. When you are feeling you are out of touch with life, return to your original voice. Listening acknowledges that there is something of great importance to hear. Listen and know the answers will come.

"What is it you long to do?" is a question I often ask clients. I want to know what they are yearning for. The first response I am often given is, "I don't know." Upon further reflection, however, the answers are known. Those answers come with stillness and listening. The key is to turn down the volume on your Inner Critic so you can hear what your desires are. Listen for what you are truly yearning. The quieter you become the more you can hear.

What do you long for?

*"Togetherness fuses Souls."*

## Soul R<sub>x</sub> #53

## *Everyone Needs To Belong*

I have been in an informal writing group for a year and a half. One person is interested in coaching the inner writer out of people. The other person and I are interested in writing a book. Let's be clear. We call ourselves a writing group, but it is interjected by food, therapy and some occasional booze. Every meeting begins with food. You cannot be creative on an empty stomach. Chocolate always insists on showing up and laughter rides shotgun. We share what we write which often leads to a personal therapy session. We help each other work something out or just listen. We are understanding without tolerating a pity party.

When we meet, we often post pictures of our meetings on social media. The fun we are having comes through the status updates loud and clear. In one particular update, my friend shared a photo of us seated at my kitchen table with a plate of chocolate chip cookies placed in the middle of the table. One of the comments wanted to know what kind of cookies we were eating. I laugh at the simplicity of the comments because they not about writing, but about how we are connecting and how much fun we are having while connecting. I claim we should name ourselves the "Tea, Cookies and Connection Club." I think that is what people really want, connection with a warm beverage and a treat. Everyone should experience connection on a regular basis. Togetherness fuses Souls.

Everyone should have a group comprised of people with whom you can be completely yourself. Be with people who make you feel safe in every way: safe to create, safe to express your true feelings, safe to show up and be real without judgement. Connection is your fuel. There is no need to suffer with loneliness or disconnection. If you do not have connection in your life, create it. Create a group around something you love to do. Connecting with people with whom you have something in common fills you up.

What would belonging to a group do for you?

**GREATNESS**

*"Taking responsibility for your life answers the call of your Highest Self."*

## Soul R<sub>x</sub> #54

## *Take Responsibility For Your Life*

There was a time when I felt really lost. I was a stay at home mom, but knew there was something more for me to do. I was feeling miserable as I tried to figure it out. I looked to my husband hoping he might have a clue what I should do. Honestly, I think I partially blamed him for not knowing what I should do with my life. You would think that if you lived with someone long enough, it would be clear to the other person. The truth? It was not his job to make me happy or to show me the way. He could support me, but he could not do the work for me. It was solely my job to find my way.

I had been out of the work world for awhile, so I had lost my confidence. I was scared. I knew I had to put myself back out there, but how? I decided to do something outside of caring for my children. I saw an ad for Toastmasters in my community newspaper. It advertised that Toastmasters could grow your communication and leadership skills. I wanted to grow in both these areas so, I decided to join. I remember driving up to the red brick high school where the meetings were held. I considered circling the school and returning home. I was terrified to put myself out there again. Meeting new people was a little scary, I could feel all my insecurities rise up. I could not have picked a scarier activity with which to begin. Most people would rather die than public speak, but I kept feeling the nudge to do this, so I had to try. No one could attend the meetings for me. If I wanted to grow in leadership and communication skills, it was all on me. I had this secret desire to be a motivational speaker, so I had to start the journey. I had to own the journey. Joining Toastmasters was one of the best things I did. It helped increase my confidence and laid the foundation for the professional work in the years that followed.

Only you can make the life you want. Take 100% responsibility for your life and include everything. Be responsible for what you say, what you do, what energy you bring, what you believe, the company you keep, what you eat, how you spend money, how much you have grown personally…everything. It is your greatest job to lead your life well.

When you stop blaming your life on external circumstances and people, you start getting somewhere. Your life is a projected image of your thinking, so you can stop pointing fingers at others. When you stop the blame game, you have come to the realization that the life you want lies solely in your hands. You have always been in charge. That's exciting. Move from the passenger seat to the driver's seat in life. Start directing where you want your life to go and decide who will accompany you on your journey.

Like a ship, you cannot change direction quickly, but you can slowly and methodically move in a new direction if you desire. Luckily, you are flexible, adaptable and moveable. Who says you could not revolutionize your life in days and weeks? Certainly in a year. Get going. How many success stories do you need to read about or watch on social media before you create one of your own?

You have choices and decisions to make, not only about what you can do in life, but who you want to be. When you decide to take personal responsibility for your life, you have answered the call of your Highest Self. Now amazing things will start to happen.

What do you need to start taking responsibility for?

*"Imagination is the breeding ground where your dreams take root."*

## Soul R<sub>x</sub> #55

## Create A Compelling Vision For Your Life

Get excited about your life. If your response to this statement is I have nothing to get excited about, you do not have a compelling vision for your life. How do you get a compelling vision?

Begin with possibility. Realize that dreams, desires and plans are possible for you. When you see possibility, you have hope that your life can be better than it is right now. When you see possibility, desire stirs within you prompting action. When you see possibility, you can achieve different outcomes for your life. Do not settle for a comfortable life. Comfortable is easy. A compelling vision challenges you to grow because it requires you to activate qualities and attributes. A shift needs to happen in order to experience the joy of becoming all you were truly meant to be.

Once you acknowledge new possibilities for yourself, move to creating a vision. It is difficult to get excited about something you cannot see. Imagination is the breeding ground where your dreams take root. It is the beginning of reality. Everything in this world is created twice. Once in the mind's eye and once in reality; for example, someone had to imagine and mentally design a sofa before it was created in the physical. Your life is no different. You have free reign with your life design. Be unafraid. There are no commitments yet, just a playground to explore what you want.

How do you begin to create a vision when you are unsure of what you want? Get in the imagination mindset:

- Create a Vision Board by cutting out images and words from magazines that you like or that speak to you in some way. Do not question or edit what you are clipping. Paste these cut outs on a piece of Bristol Board. Collectively the cut outs will begin to tell your story. What does your story tell you? What desires does it reflect back? How does this visual narrative make you feel? You do know what you want. When you construct a Vision Board, you have created a life in your imagination. The real question is do you have the courage and tenacity to bring it to life?

- Answer the BIG questions such as:

    What would get you excited if you knew it could come true?
    What have you been longing to do?
    If you knew you could not fail, what would you do?
    If time and money were not an issue, what would you do?
    What is my vision board reflecting back to me?

The fun part of creating a compelling vision is exploring possibility and designing your life. It is fun to stay in the dream stage, but the magic and momentum happens when you move to action. Give yourself permission to dream big.

What does a compelling vision for your life look like?

*"You have time to change your story."*

## Soul R$_x$ #56

## Tell A New Story

Stories are powerful. When you hear a story, it has the power to move you. The stories you tell yourself are most important. They either help you or hurt you. Your stories tap into your emotions. Depending on the story you tell yourself and the world, they have the capability to influence, inspire, or move you to action or they can make you sad, small and paralyzed.

What story do you tell yourself on a regular basis? Are you an amazing, worthy person who is moving toward getting more of what you want or are you the weak character victimized by the world never getting what you want? The first story is from someone who is connected to their Highest Self. It is a story that makes you feel alive. It makes you believe the world is here to support you, that things can work out for you. The latter story is the work of your Inner Critic making you feel bad, making you afraid, and validating your fears. This trickster would love nothing more than for you to believe you are not winning in life. These stories, if not filtered out or challenged, run like rampant wildfire burning out all of your dreams, wants, and desires.

Imagine if you fell down the stairs knocking yourself unconscious then woke up not remembering anything about how you felt about a current difficulty. Having no memory of it, you would not feel bad about it. You might, however, feel appreciative of your life feeling thankful for people in your life. Without having an experience that causes amnesia, you can begin telling yourself a new story erasing the old track that has played in your head.

Stop recalling the old stories that make you feel unworthy and unwell. Start telling yourself the story that will make you feel good. Feeling good is a precursor to winning at life. The stories you tell indicate whether you are listening to your Inner Critic or your Highest Self.

You have time to change your story.

What story do you need to start telling yourself?

*"Limiting beliefs are prosperity thieves."*

## Soul R<sub>x</sub> #57

## *Remove Limiting Beliefs*

Do you sometimes wonder why you just cannot break through? Why do others seem to be so abundant and prosperous? Why do some people have all the luck? Perhaps you have suspected they have a strategically placed horseshoe. Those who know the truth, however, know prosperity is dependent on what people believe. Beliefs can either propel you forward or hold you back. What you believe becomes the truth. What you believe becomes your limit.

I have a friend that found a clever way to keep her dog from running off when the family goes camping. At home, she installed an electric dog fence to keep her dog from wandering off the property. The electric fence is an invisible boundary that is created by a wireless transmitter sending a circular signal around the yard. The dog wears a collar that receives an audible signal warning him when he approaches the boundary. If he goes through the fence, he will receive a static correction. Over time, the dog learns that he is not to exceed the established boundary. To help the dog learn his perimeter, little white flags are placed where the invisible fence is as a visual reminder. The dog learns the white flags are his limit. When my friend goes camping, she cannot take the "invisible fence" with her, but she can take the little white flags. She creates a perimeter with the little white flags around the family camper. The dog recognizes the familiar white flags as his limit. Interestingly, the dog stays within the limit of his white flags even though there is nothing stopping him from moving beyond them.

Beliefs are like the little white flags. What limiting beliefs have you become so familiar with that you cannot move beyond them even though there is nothing stopping you? Think about the different areas of your life: relationships, personal growth, career, leadership, spirituality, health, community involvement. What you achieve in these areas is dependent on what you believe. Regardless of how you learned the beliefs, they are only thoughts you think repeatedly until they become so familiar that you unknowingly adopt them as truth.

Limiting beliefs are:

*Personal statements:*
I am not good enough.
I do not have enough education.
I am not as smart as others.
I am not likeable.
I am not as good looking as others.
I did not do well in school.
I cannot get ahead.
My parents did not teach me how to be successful.
I am not young enough.

*Clichés:*
There is never enough money to go around.
Every time you make a mark somebody paints the wall.
Life is hard.
Money does not grow on trees.

Limiting beliefs are prosperity thieves. They lead you to assume that life is out to get you versus support you. The good news is new beliefs can easily be created. Prosperity is a mindset first, so shed your old beliefs and adopt new ones by creating new healthy, exciting thoughts. *Caution:* Like old habits, old beliefs die hard. Your mind will want to go to the old familiar script it has been playing. The work is in practicing new thought patterns so new beliefs can be established.

*Supportive beliefs:*
I am worthy.
I can create prosperity.
I am prosperous.
Regardless of my education or background, I am capable of living the life I choose.
I can set a new positive example of how to live an abundant life.
I have much to contribute and offer to my workplace/relationship/life.
My uniqueness is what sets me apart.
I am loveable.
I can change.
I can make new choices.

Give yourself a chance at prosperity. Make your own list of supportive statements.

What limiting beliefs do you have that steal your prosperity?

*"You cannot go around it; you have to go through it."*

## Soul R<sub>x</sub> #58

## Get In The Game

I never played sports growing up, so when I decided to take up golf, I had no confidence to play it. After I joined a Golf Club, I made a plan. I decided that I would spend six weeks hanging out on the driving range and putting greens practicing and learning. Six weeks seemed like the perfect number to learn how to get good at this sport. I told myself, an actual golf game was for people who knew how to play. I really did not think you would *play* golf if you did not know how to do it. I did not want to look foolish.

I had a friend who belonged to the same Golf Club. Within days of joining, she immediately asked me to play a round with her. When she called to invite me, I voiced my concerns to her, "I can't play. I don't know how." She busted my six week learning plan. She convinced me to play a round of golf with her. We played nine holes. I was tired and exhausted, but I had played my first round of golf. I soon realized that the only way to learn was by playing golf not practicing it off the course. If I had refused to play that day I would not have gotten in the game. I began where I was at the very beginning of the learning curve. You can begin where you are. Just because you do not know how to do something does not mean you cannot begin. You have to begin if you want to learn, grow and get better. You cannot go around it; you have to go through it.

Practicing is good, but getting in the game is better. Golf has taught me that.

Consider moving from...

- the passenger seat in life to the driver's seat.
- practicing to playing.
- watching to doing.
- consuming to producing.
- practicing to performing.
- hiding to being seen.
- thinking to acting.
- theory to reality.
- knowledge to execution.
- inspiration to engagement.
- the back of the room to the front of the room.
- participating to leading.

There is no substitute for doing. It is through action you learn.

Where are you not "getting in the game?"

*"There are many roads to where you want to go."*

## Soul R<sub>x</sub> #59

## *There Are Many Paths To Greatness*

One day, in the midst of my domestic Goddess work, my husband arrived home from a course where he learned about using coaching in the workplace. He was inspired by the woman, Jane, who led the course. My husband passionately pointed his finger at me and said, "This was you. This woman was you. This is what you are supposed to be doing." As I rocked a child back and forth on my hip, I said, "That's great, but I don't know what to do about it." I did not know what coaching was or how to become a coach. It did not mean anything to me. I could, however, feel the passion and genuine connection he had made between what this woman was doing for a living and what he envisioned me doing.

Of course, his passion made me curious about this woman. How did she become a coach? He explained that Jane was a psychologist and had worked on domestic abuse cases by accompanying police on their calls. One evening she got shot while accompanying police on one of those calls. Wanting a safer line of work, she then began teaching coaching to leaders in a University setting. I internalized Jane's path as the path to coaching. I believed how Jane found coaching was how I must find coaching. First, I needed to earn a psychology degree, have a major life shift by getting shot on the job then teach at a University and ta-da, I can become a coach. I instantly assumed coaching was not going to be an option because I could not travel Jane's path. This was simply not true.

I would eventually find my own journey to coaching. As my last child approached school age, I started to wonder what would be next for me.

On a girls weekend away, friends who knew a Life Coach suggested I reach out to her to get help figuring out a new path. It was one of the most powerful set of conversations I would ever have. After a few months of being coached, I decided to become a Life Coach. I signed up for my first coaching course which launched me into a new industry and on a whole new path. This path expanded to include knowing more people who are coaches. I learned to teach coaching too. It is very fulfilling work. I could never have imagined that I would find coaching in the way that I did. It was my path and very different from Jane's.

Your greatness is waiting for you on your path. Search your heart for what you really want to do in this life. Even if you want a job or life that is similar to someone else's, refrain from thinking that how someone else got to their destination is the only way. It is not. There are many roads to where you want to go. Your job is to define what you want in life and begin moving in that direction. The path will be revealed to you.

What have you been longing to do?

*"Lack of courage keeps you on a short leash."*

## Soul R<sub>x</sub> #60

## *Choose Your Dream Life*

Most people are living the life they have the courage to live right now. It is a real life that is mostly safe and comfortable. It is one where you walk through life wearing a set of bumper pads navigating life with as little rejection, disappointment and hurt as possible. However, many people have another life: their dream life. It is the life they wish they had the courage to live. It is a life dreamed in colour, where many exciting possibilities exist.

The life I am living on a daily basis right now is the one I have the courage to live. In my dream life, however, I have opened and closed a bakery and a dessert café. I have been a bestselling author and songwriter. I have learned guitar and piano flawlessly. I have been an international motivational speaker. None of which to this point have come true. Although, I can say, I am inching toward some of my dreams.

Your dream life runs parallel to the one you are currently living. It contains juicy dreams. When you think of them, it makes you come alive inside or scare you completely. Dreams connect you to your Soul. Many never make the leap to living out their desires choosing instead to stay close to the shore of certainty. It is easier to be safe because going for your dreams means being vulnerable, taking risks, revealing yourself, overcoming your insecurities, moving beyond your limiting beliefs, and being the subject of other's discussions. It is truly putting yourself out there.

Lack of courage keeps you on a short leash, but when you choose to continuously reach into your dream life to bring an idea to fruition, you bridge the gap between who you are and who you want to be. All dreams are held in escrow until you have the courage to release them. You know there are dreams that exist within you. Have the courage to choose your dream life. When you partner with courage, you partner with your Highest Self.

What dreams do you want to bring into reality?

*"Do not steal your joy before it arrives."*

## Soul R<sub>x</sub> #61

## Live In A State of Great Expectation

Do you hold the belief that if life is getting too good something bad must be coming down the pipeline because you believe life does not just give you goodness? This is a fear mindset. When you live in fear, you block opportunities, prosperity, friendships and connection from arriving. Do you question and doubt the good things that show up? When you assume something bad is lurking around the corner, you steal your joy before it arrives.

Living in a state of great expectation means you are making space for goodness to come to you. Living in a state of great expectation means you are replacing fear with excitement. Great expectation is a signal that you want goodness to show up. You are saying "I'm ready." Once you have activated great expectation, something magical happens. Expectation acts like a magnet drawing to you what you desire. Activate and hold the state of expectation and watch what happens.

You want more prosperity?  **Expect it.**
You want more opportunity?  **Expect it.**
You want more goodness?  **Expect it.**
You want better health?  **Expect it.**

Expectation is not about creating demands or feeling like you deserve it, but it does mean holding a mindset that clears the channel to receive all that you desire. Living in a state of great expectation means living in a state of no doubt. Expectation moves you toward what you want. Doubt moves you away from it. Which direction do you want to move?

Your Highest Self is calling out to you to raise your level of expectation.

What are you expecting to happen?

*"Downplaying who you are is shunning your greatness."*

## *Soul R<sub>x</sub> #62*

## *Step Into Your Greatness*

I have written resumes to help people in career transition. At the top of the resume, I would write a Profile Statement which is equivalent to a 30 second elevator pitch selling the candidate to a potential employer. The Profile Statement would highlight the person's education, strengths, qualities, abilities and achievements. It always astounded me the number of people who thought the statement I constructed sounded too big for them. The statement embarrassed some even making them blush. I would check with them to confirm that what I had written was the truth about them. They would always agree that what they had to offer is what I had explained on paper. The clients, however, still challenged me, "Does that sound too big?" or "Does it sound like I am bragging?" My clients shunned who they were and what they had to offer the world.

I was equally amazed at those whose greatness I captured on paper who absolutely loved what I wrote. Reading back to clients what I had written, some reactions were priceless, "Wow! I sound great. I'd hire me." I assured them that they were great. When you show people who they are, you help build their confidence. Where there is confidence, success follows.

People have blind spots for their greatness. They can easily pick out what is good about others, but cannot see it in themselves. When you reflect back to people their greatness, it lifts them up. People walk away feeling good about themselves.

When you say "I am not that good" or "I don't have much to offer," you push away your greatness. Do not downplay your greatness. It keeps you from good jobs, good friends, good spouses, and good opportunities. This is not about bragging. This is about acceptance and appreciation of who you are and what you have to offer. Embrace it. Being hard on yourself is easy. Being gentle on yourself is self-love.

Step into your greatness by appreciating and accepting:

- what you have achieved
- your qualities
- how far you have come
- your personality
- your quirks
- what lights you up
- your skills

Your Highest Self is calling on you to use your greatness in this world. It is needed. Step into it and use it to launch you forward.

What is great about you?

*"You give your power away to difficult situations, but you can take your power back."*

## Soul R$_x$ #63

## *Put Down The Heavy Baggage*

No one is immune to difficult or unsettling situations. The situation may be in the past, but often what gets carried forward is the negative thoughts, feelings and energy around it. You carry the emotional residue as if you are carrying pieces of heavy luggage. You become drained of your precious energy in the present by carrying the baggage from the past. If you recall an experience from your past that upset you, I bet you can create a very good rant in your head around who wronged you, how you felt, and how frustrated you were. I would bet money your body becomes tense moving from peace to disturbed in seconds. What's worse? Every time you talk about the experience, you give it momentum making the story bigger and maybe seem even worse than it was. Put down the heavy baggage. It is too costly a price to pay.

Carrying around unnecessary baggage from the past robs you of joy and happiness because it keeps you in the experience. Putting down the baggage means releasing the negative energy you hold around the upsetting experience. It is a shift in perspective. It means that you are willing to create a shift so that it no longer holds power over you.

Decide to get the lesson and move on. Do not give the old situation any more attention or power. You give your power away to difficult situations, but you can take your power back. Taking your power back is living from the space of your Highest Self where your joy resides. When you value your joy, you will do anything to keep it. You do not have to stay miserable and upset. Putting down the baggage is an act of self-love.

What past situations do you need to release?

*"Your talent is sitting dormant waiting for you to activate it."*

## Soul R$_x$ #64

## *There Is No Cap On Your Potential*

One day our family took a short road trip. Our two teenaged kids were begrudgingly riding along in the back seat. At the time, I was in the middle of writing this book. During the drive another book idea came to me. I thought for fun and to find a way to connect with my kids as we drove, I would ask my kids for some input on this new idea. As I made my request, my twelve year old daughter pipes up from the backseat to make a clarification. These ideas are for another book, not the one you are currently writing? I said, "That's correct." She was not concerned about making a contribution. She was curious. She asked me, "How many books do you intend to write?" I replied, "Probably fifty." From the backseat I hear, "Pffft," pass her lips as if to sarcastically say, "Yeah, right." Fifty books sounds like a lot to a twelve year old. It is a big number. It sounds ridiculous actually, especially, if you have not even finished writing one book.

Who knows if I will actually write fifty books, but I feel like there is a lot inside me waiting to be written. The only way to write forty nine more is to write the first one. Life is not about achieving your goals; it is about reaching for your potential. Writing a book is a goal, but who I have to become to write it demands me to live up to my potential. My potential demanded a commitment to park myself to write for many days. It demanded an ability to write. I wrote my way out of many ideas. As I wrote, my writing potential shifted. I got stronger and better. My potential demanded me to reflect, connect and work with ideas I wanted to communicate. As a result, reflection got richer and ideas flowed more easily. I am a different person at the end of writing this book than I was when I started it. As I wrote, my potential moved.

As you reach your potential, it shifts, forcing you to grow again. Who I will be when I begin writing my second book is very different from who I was when I started writing my first book.

In your life, you never have to worry about arriving. Life is a continuous unfolding of your potential. Your potential dangles in front of you like a carrot hanging from a stick encouraging you to keep growing. If you want all the great things in life (fulfillment, happiness, money, recognition, connection) you have to work toward your potential. Perhaps you are wanting a certain job for which you are not qualified. Develop your talent and skills to get the job you want. Your talent is sitting dormant waiting for you to activate it. Honing your talent then becomes a stepping stone to another opportunity. That is how potential works. As you grow, your potential moves. Potential is an ever shifting line.

Rest assured that there is always an opportunity to work toward your potential. If you feel like you are out of opportunity or feel stagnant, you are not tapped out. Your potential is waiting on you. You have to make the first move. You will feel so good about yourself when you start moving toward your potential. No matter what age, you can start growing again. There are no restrictions on achieving potential.

What feels like the next natural step to activate your potential?

*"Difficulties present us with opportunities to be better versions of ourselves."*

## Soul R$_x$ #65

### *Intensity Reveals Your Brilliance*

Our house is a crafting house. My daughter is compelled to create daily. It could be painting, converting tinfoil into a sculpture, creating a binder cover or trying experiments. My daughter could personally kick-start the economy with the money she spends at craft stores. Last summer, she tried painting pottery for the first time. As we entered through the doors of the business, we were overwhelmed by the vibrant painted walls as well as the colourful tables and chairs. Displayed on the floor to ceiling shelves were chalky, ceramic figures waiting to be painted.

My daughter chose a small moose to paint. The best part of painting pottery is using your imagination to choose colours to bring the dull, plain ceramic figures to life. My daughter stood before the array of colours on the wall considering her options. The shop owner approached us to explain the colour choices. The owner pointed out that the paint colours displayed on the small white tiles on the wall were different from what appeared in the paint bottles. The paint colours on the wall showed how the colours appear after being fired in a kiln under high heat. The colours in the paint bottles were dull. The shop owner explained that only when a painted ceramic piece is subjected to intense heat are the true colours revealed. A muted mauve changes to bright pink. A sandy, milk chocolate converts to dark brown.

You are like an unfinished piece of pottery. Life subjects you to intense situations. It is only under intensity that your true brilliance is revealed.

Think of situations, although difficult, that made you better:

- You came through a difficult divorce to find that you were stronger than you knew.

- You walked a difficult road with another only to find your path.

- You were treated badly by another, but you held yourself to the spiritual high road showing your beautiful spirit.

- You were passed over for a job, only to find yourself working harder to get what you want.

- You experienced difficulties in business forcing you to find the courage to become the leader you needed to be.

Difficulties present us with opportunities to be better versions of ourselves - richer, brighter and shinier.

What difficulty have you been subjected to that has made you shine brilliantly?

**MINDSET**

*"Spending time is transactional; investing time is transformational."*

## Soul R<sub>x</sub> #66

## *You Are The Company You Keep*

You can tell a lot about a person by how they spend their time and with whom they spend their time. Know that the people you associate with on a regular basis greatly influence you. If you have great dreams waiting to be birthed, evaluate who is in your closest circle to help support you and encourage you. The likelihood of birthing your dreams is dependent on the quality of your inner most circle.

Begin to recognize time as a valuable key to making the most of your days. Shift from the idea of spending time to investing time. Spending time is transactional; investing time is transformational. Investing time means surrounding yourself with people who lift you up, not let you down; challenging you to grow instead of convincing you to give up; bring out your best versus focusing on your shortcomings. When you spend time, it is gone. When you invest time with others, you get a return on that investment: joy, information, a collaborative business partner, a rich friendship, connection.

It is costly to spend time with the time vampires who want to expend your time and energy to complain, gossip, use you as a dumpsite for their negative energy or want you to constantly save them. If you are not getting your needs met in a group, it is time to find a new group. Time is valuable because you cannot create more of it. Everyone is given the same number of hours in a day. How will you spend your time?

There are people in your life, including family members, that can be huge time vampires that you can place into the "minimal contact" category. You cannot avoid them completely, but you must distance yourself from them. Decide how you will manage the time with them, otherwise they will decide for you. There is a price to pay when you leave your precious time in the hands of others.

Connection with others is one of the best ways to grow. Become highly conscious of the company you keep because you will be influenced by the people with whom you most associate. Make a list of the people with whom you spend the most time. With each person, evaluate whether you are spending time or investing time.

What are you getting from the company you keep?

*"You have much to offer this world."*

## Soul R<sub>x</sub> #67

## *Validate All Experiences*

Everything you have done in your life counts. Nothing is ever wasted. Years ago I joined Toastmasters to improve my public speaking skills. Toastmasters' mentors tell you to write about what you know, but I often struggled with finding something on which to speak. One evening, I participated in a teleseminar with very successful speakers who gave great tips about how to get speech ideas. They asked questions such as:

What special knowledge do you have?
What are your hobbies?
What is your work experience?
What are you passionate about?
What are your dreams?

What I realized is that I had more things to talk about than I had given myself credit. As I answered each of the questions, stories began to pop into my head. The teleseminar leaders said, "Validate all experiences." It was a brilliant statement because it underscored the point that you take for granted what you already know. You tend to overlook or discount what you have to offer the world. Every job, every ounce of education, every hobby, every passion, every quality, every skill, every conversation, and every conflict serves to add to your uniqueness.

Acknowledge that you have a wide spectrum of talents and skills that often go unaccounted for or dismissed because you assign it no value. I earned a Bachelor of Education at University, but spent little time teaching in the school system choosing instead to work in the corporate world. I remember someone saying to me, "It's too bad you're not using your education." I was annoyed by this statement because the person was dismissing everything I had learned in achieving a degree. Furthermore, I would not have been offered a job in the corporate world had I not earned a degree. My education brought me financial gain, gave me credibility that I could achieve, expanded my worldview and pointed me in the direction of my purpose. Becoming a teacher indicated to me that I was a teacher at the core whether I ever taught in a school system or not. This ability to help others can be translated into other areas.

Here is another example of not discounting the small things you do. My son has many interests: learning new music to play on the piano, solving puzzles and inventing. One day I asked him what did all these things have in common. Without even thinking about it, he said, "I like to solve problems and I like to work with my hands." All these seemingly regular experiences and interests are perhaps pointing him toward his career or calling in life. He alluded to becoming a surgeon. He could also be a mechanic or an engineer or a musician. Who knows?

Playing piano, solving puzzles and inventing are activities, but it is what lies beneath these activities that is important. The activities that bring my son joy point him to his strengths and values. These activities highlight that he likes creativity, problem solving and working with patterns. This is valuable information as he chooses how to make a living.

Do not overlook the small activities that bring you joy. Be conscious of what you are doing and what strengths and skills you are employing when lose track of time. The small things are pointing you to the big things; they are telling you stories of who you are.

All experiences are valuable. They are degrees in the human experience. Use them to deepen your connection with yourself and pay attention to what they are telling you. They are carving out a path for you to follow. You have much to offer this world. Your path or purpose may be discreetly wrapped in the package of the ordinary. Validate all experiences.

What have you dismissed that can point you to your uniqueness?

*"Positivity is an ongoing conscious, spiritual practice."*

## Soul R<sub>x</sub> #68

## *Positive Thinking Is A Practice*

Thoughts come into your mind constantly like a live streaming television program. Not certain about that? Test this by sitting still for a few moments. Notice the frequency of your thoughts. What might even shock you more is the quality of your thoughts. You may, in fact, be stuck on the negativity channel. Only when you can become conscious of this unchecked behaviour, can you shift yourself away from the negative and into the positive.

What does negative thinking look like? It looks like judgement, exasperation, frustration, jealousy, criticism, guilt, worry, righteousness, fear. As you become aware of the quality of your thoughts, attune yourself to how they make you feel. If you leave your stream of consciousness on the negativity channel, nothing in your life looks or feels right. You will begin to question everything in your life. You may even physically manifest symptoms as a result of negative thoughts.

Your life follows your thoughts. The best way to stop negative momentum is to express gratitude and appreciation. These are powerful practices that change the direction of your momentum. Movement in the positive direction is only a small shift away.

Convert and reframe thoughts until you develop a positive habit of thinking. Positivity is the playbook of the Highest Self. Positivity is an ongoing conscious, spiritual practice. Change the channel to positivity.

When do you struggle to be positive?

*"You are always only one shift away from feeling better."*

## Soul R$_x$ #69

## *A Mind Shift Is A Life Shift*

You are always only one shift away from feeling better. Shifts can be created through your thought process. If you want sustainable joy, practice thinking new thoughts about your life. Imagine thoughts are like bubbles. They can be light, airy, and fragile, but they can also feel heavy and controlling. Like bubbles, you can burst the thoughts that make you feel unwell. Choose to fill your mind with thought bubbles that lift your spirit.

Read the list of negative thoughts below. Now read the list of positive thoughts.

| **Negative Thoughts** | **Positive Thoughts** |
| --- | --- |
| I'm scared to make a mistake. | Today is a good day. |
| I'm too old to start a business. | I have a lot to offer this world. |
| Everyone is happy, but me. | I have many great qualities. |
| Nothing ever works out for me. | It is never too late for me to start something. |
| I am not where I want to be. | I am grateful for many things in my life. |
| I don't get opportunities. | I can turn my life around with small changes. |
| My life is falling apart. | I have people who love me. |

Notice the difference in how you feel when you read each list. Good thoughts make you feel good. Bad thoughts make you feel bad. Thoughts are the difference maker. Consistently thinking good thoughts shifts your life. When you shift your thinking, your life shifts.

Hold positive thoughts that support you. Your life follows your thoughts.

What mindset do you hold most often?

*"Your peace is threatened when drama is lurking."*

## Soul R$_x$ #70

## Opt Out Of Drama

Drama is an addiction for many people. If those addicted to drama are not creating it, they know how to find it. If the drama barometer is low, they know how to crank it up. Drama is like a drug that you slowly become addicted to eventually not knowing how to exist without it. Drama takes the form of gossip, complaints, manipulations, taking things personally, spinning stories, misinterpretations, assumptions and a general negative approach to life. Drama is seductive as it draws attention to you and increases self-importance.

Drama:

- drains you of positive energy
- removes your ability to be grateful
- extinguishes hope about life and people
- robs your inspiration to chase dreams
- forces you to play small
- sees conflict where there is none

Drama is practiced. You can unlearn how to be a drama queen or king. You do not want to be that person who continuously focuses on problems even when good solutions are presented. When you exist in the space of drama too long, anything else seems unnatural. The antidote to drama is awareness. Become super conscious of how you are living your daily life. How much drama do you create or get pulled into?

You may not be the creator of the drama, but it is equally disastrous to participate in it because it gives drama fuel to rage out of control like a wildfire. Your peace is threatened when drama is lurking. Protect your peace with fierce determination. You disconnect with your Highest Self when you participate in drama.

Opt of out of drama. Stay in peace.

When do you feel yourself creating or participating in drama?

*"When you always do your best, you stand out."*

## Soul R$_x$ #71

## *Always Do Your Best*

Excellence is a spiritual practice that aligns your Inner Being with your Outer Being. When you align with your Highest Self, excellence is enabled. Excellence is a way of being that paves a path to opportunity.

When I was fresh out of university, I could not find a teaching job and the bills had to get paid, so I took a job as an Administrative Assistant. I did not have the experience working in an administrative position, but I knew how to deliver excellence. Although I feared I would not measure up to the job, I arrived at work early, had a good attitude, displayed a friendly disposition, did more than I was asked, anticipated needs, and helped internal and external customers in any way I could. After eight months, I had my first review which was very much in my favour. They gave me an $8000 raise and a lump sum cheque for an amount retro to my start date. I was pleased knowing my work ethic and attitude had paid off, literally. Excellence draws more opportunity to you.

Being excellent is a personal philosophy for success. When you always do your best, you stand out. You never know who is watching you. It could be a current employer, a future client or a collaborative partner. Doing your best blazes a trail to more opportunity. Embrace excellence as a way of being.

What does your personal best look like?

*"What you take from your experience becomes your story."*

## Soul R$_x$ #72

## *Create Your Story*

No doubt you have had your fair share of difficulties and challenges.

- you are divorced.
- you are a child of divorce.
- you had a falling out with your family.
- you were passed over for a promotion.
- your child is struggling.
- your business is floundering.
- you were abandoned.
- you were bullied.
- you came from a financially challenged family.
- you struggle with your thoughts.

Check in with yourself about the difficulties you have suffered. What have you taken away from your experiences? What stories do you tell the world about your difficulties? Are you always the victim? Do you tell stories as proof that life is not working out for you? If you are divorced, do you think of yourself as broken or damaged goods? Your marriage broke, but you are not broken. Divorce is what happened to you, but that is not who you are. Refrain from negatively labelling yourself. What is the positive story that you can project into the world? Everyone encounters circumstances that challenge, frighten, or frustrate. Like a producer of a television show, you create the story that you tell the world about your experiences. How you recount your stories is a sign of how you exited your experiences. What you take from your experience becomes your story. You give power to that which you give attention.

What story are you telling the world about you?

*"Beauty is found in moments."*

## Soul R<sub>x</sub> #73

## *See The Beauty In Every Day*

Seeing the beauty in everyday is a practice of being in the present moment. On social media, people regularly update their status by hitting the "check in" button to announce where they are having dinner or what gym they are at. Checking into social media is a purposeful act. Take the same few moments used to update your social media status to check into your life. Seize the daily opportunity to scan your life. Purposefully check in.

My mother is not well. Most days she stays in bed to rest. Day after day, she is immersed in the same surroundings. As I sit with her on her bed, I watch how she examines her hands. As I watch her looking at her hand, I revere the beauty of the human body. The amazing ability for hands to move on invisible command. I see the beauty of the fine creases on the back of her hand that look like a sketch. I recognize, too, the beauty that is found in the still moments between us.

Do not get so wrapped up in the smallness of life that you miss the beauty in everyday. Beauty surrounds you. It is found in the eyes of your children, the unconditional love of your pet, the roaring of the ocean, the kindness between people, an exchange between two people in love, expressed friendship, or watching a garden come to life. Beauty is found in moments. When you lift your head, beauty will always be staring back. The question is whether you can see it or not.

Shifting to the space of your Highest Self allows you to see the beauty in everyday.

What beauty are you missing?

*"Opportunity shows you what you value."*

## Soul R$_x$ #74

## *Use The Opportunities That Lie Before You*

When opportunity comes knocking, it is exciting. Opportunity fires up excitement in your life because it holds within it a seed of possibility. It is nice to have opportunity, but what if you have to say no to it even if you really want it?

An amazing business opportunity was delivered to my husband and me. It was a life changer. The upside of owning this particular business would have brought professional and financial success which was what we wanted. It required, however, uprooting our family to start over in a new community. The children were not excited about that. I certainly did not love the idea of uprooting. For a week, we grappled with the decision. It caused us to re-examine our life. What did we really want? What would be the impact on our kids? What would our lives look like five years from now? How could we make this work? We looked at it from every angle, but we were not ultimately able to say "yes." We turned down the opportunity. It is difficult to say no when the upside of the opportunity is so good. Saying no actually felt like a loss.

The decision caused emotional upheaval. Opportunity is supposed to be a good thing, I thought. I was upset that opportunity even came into our life rearing its smiling, shiny face. This was not a challenge where we had to find the silver lining. It was an opportunity! Good things come from opportunity.

Saying no to the opportunity forced deep reflection on why this was so difficult to turn down. If adversity comes to grow you, then what does an opportunity that you really want and have to say no to supposed to teach you? The answer: opportunity shows you what you value. We value the life we built. We value the connection with friends. We value having our children continue growing up in a town where they now have roots. We value the quality of life where we live. Bottom line, we value connection, community, and quality of life over financial success. This is why the decision was so hard. We wanted the exciting new opportunity, but the things we valued more won. Values provide clarity in decision making.

Opportunity also forced us to listen to our intuition. Our heads were saying yes, but our hearts were saying no. We both struggled with saying no because our Inner Critics reared their ugly heads scaring us to believe there may not be any more opportunities like this. This may be the only shot we get at success. Our Inner Critics warned us opportunities were not plentiful where we live. The great internal struggle was caused by our belief that there was only ONE opportunity that could give us what we want. This was simply not true.

I reflected deeply on how this opportunity affected us. Turning down the opportunity allowed us to see other opportunities that were right in front of us. There is never just one opportunity. There was one opportunity highlighted. There is never just one path. Practice seeing opportunities. Examine your life for opportunities that you can turn into gold. They are present, but you need to train yourself to see them. What opportunities are lying right in front of you? Capitalize on the ones that resonate with what you value. Finding the opportunity is the easy part. Opportunities only provide starting points for your dreams. What you do with them is what matters. Regardless of the path, it takes effort turning opportunity to gold.

What opportunities lie before you that you are overlooking?

*"Failure does not take you farther from your goal,
it brings you closer to it."*

## Soul R$_x$ #75

## *Reframe Failure*

Failure can be a scary word. No one wants to be considered a failure. Most prefer to be a success. Those who have claimed success, however, came to it through failure. If the idea of failure is holding you back, it is time to reframe the way you look at it.

Think of failure as:

- **a learning opportunity.** Just because you are not winning does not mean you are not learning. At university I took many English courses. Although I had done well in high school, I received grades of C, C+ and B minus on my papers for the first two years of University. I considered this failure. In high school, I had been a solid English student, so this was upsetting to me. I could not figure it out. My writing had not changed since high school. Turns out that was the problem. I really never knew how to write well. How professors graded in university was much different than how high school teachers graded papers. In my third year, I had an American Literature professor who helped turn my writing around. He gave me specific feedback on how to improve. I paid attention to his feedback and applied it each time I wrote a new paper. What began to happen? I started receiving better marks on my papers. This was a very memorable turning point for me in my writing. I never forgot the lessons my professor taught me. Experiencing this difficulty was one of the best things that could have happened to me. I never would have improved had I not experienced failure in this area. You learn more by failing than winning, yet so many are afraid of failing or being labeled a failure. If you are afraid to fail, you are afraid to learn.

- **a necessary part of success.** Success leaves clues; failure is one of them. Shift from thinking of the experience as "Too bad I failed" to "Yeah. I failed!" Failure does not take you farther from your goal, it brings you closer to it. Failure is not something to avoid, it is the way.

- **feedback or a result.** Failure must be on the path to success because it gives you great feedback. It teaches you what you have to learn and where you need to grow. It tells you when to course correct. Make the correction and move on without holding onto the idea of failure.

- **a statement about your goal, not a statement about you.** Failure is neither a judgment nor an opinion of you or your worthiness. You failed at something, but you are not a failure. Understand the difference.

- **something you need to talk more about.** Everyone has failed in some way: a test; a project that did not turn out the way you wanted; you lost money; you did not get picked for the school play; you did not make the sports team. Those who succeeded, first had failures. When you share your failures, others will too. In fact, they will be relieved. Furthermore, stories about failures and setbacks make better stories.

Failure is a matter of perspective. Reframe how you look at failure, so you can ease into action. Fear of failure keeps you from starting your dreams. When you detach yourself from failure, you establish connection with your Highest Self.

How would reframing your perspective on failure help you?

# *AUTHENTICITY*

*"Being authentic is your gift to the world."*

## Soul R$_x$ #76

## *Be Authentic*

Authenticity is about who you are being. To be authentic is to show the world who you are. It is to give birth to the divine spark that is within you. Living an authentic life makes a courageous statement to the world that you know who you are, you love who you are and you are willing to birth the real you into the world. Being authentic is effortless and fearless.

Does the world know who you are, truly? Or do you live out a small version of yourself? Playing small is like being locked in a prison waiting for someone to set you free, but you are the only one who has the key. Your Highest Self constantly nudges you to show up in life, to bring your gifts to the world. The nudges may appear as thoughts or desires, "I would love to try that" or your attention keeps being drawn to an idea or similar opportunities repeatedly show up. Maybe you constantly receive feedback from others telling you, "I can see you doing that." Your Highest Self is always fiercely calling you forth asking more of you because you have so much potential. Try new activities regardless of the outcome. Do things that scare you (fear can show you what you want). Reveal your thoughts, create and share. You were not birthed into this world to play the small version of you. Pay attention to the nudges.

It is exhausting to continually show up as something you are not. Living in alignment with your Highest Self is to live authentically. Once you know who you are, you cannot ignore it. Being authentic is a giant step to true freedom. Choosing to live authentically draws out the authenticity in others. When you decide to show up authentically, it gives others the courage to do the same. Authenticity is powerful.

Reconnecting with your Highest Self is a constant return home. You falter and reconnect. You get misaligned and reconnect. Do not give up on yourself. Being authentic is your gift to the world.

Where are you playing small in your life?

*"Another's comfortableness allows you to be comforted."*

## Soul R$_x$ #77

## *Achieve Authentic Connection*

Authenticity is an inside job. It is easier to find authentic connections with others when you already have it with yourself. Work at getting in touch with your Highest Self. Make your spiritual connection a priority. When you are willing to live authentically, you attract authenticity.

Have you ever heard yourself or others say, "She is so comfortable in her own skin." You recognize authenticity. Those people are in touch with their Inner Being. They may not even realize it. They have learned to move through life without a lot of resistance, their Ego, weighing them down. They do not spend time fabricating stories about themselves or others. They show up and get on with life.

You can feel when someone is being authentic because you are feeling in them the same part that is also inside you. You know when you are achieving authentic connection. Authentic people are easy to be around. Their presence encourages your authenticity to step forward. They provide a safe passage for you to be yourself. You feel less guarded in their presence. Authentic people are really good at seeing the light in others.

Another's comfortableness allows you to be comforted.

With whom do you feel authentic connection?

*"Values kick the door wide open to discovering who you are."*

## Soul R<sub>x</sub> #78

## *Know What You Value*

Lives are often built on doing by stockpiling achievements. You graduate from high school, obtain secondary education, get a career, start a business, find a mate, get married, have children, volunteer. You become great at getting focused on the doing side of life. At some point, you may begin to experience a restlessness like something is missing even though you have many things going well for you. Life may seem uninspiring or joyless. Your tendency may be to switch things up such as changing jobs, ending relationships, or buying things only to find yourself still in the same lackluster boat.

Knowing what your Internal Values are, however, is a secret road to joy and fulfillment. There are two types of values: Internal Values and External Values. There are many things that you may value in life such as your job, money, status, your home. These are External Values. Nothing wrong with that. They are valuable. Many people want these, but they rarely create true fulfillment. To truly know yourself, however, is to know your Internal Values. Internal Values answer "Who am I? It is a way of viewing yourself from the inside out. Internal Values can help you be more focused and informed about choosing what you DO in this life which leads to greater joy and fulfillment. Your being informs your doing. Internal Values lead you to your External Values. If you want that job, car, home, position at work, who do you have to BE in order to achieve it?

Answering the question "Who Am I?" can be overwhelming. I can remember the first time I struggled with that question as a result of defining myself from the external. To complete my Bachelor of Education degree, I had to assume the responsibilities of a teacher. For four months, I taught and built relationships with teachers and students. Students looked to me for guidance and I contributed as part of the staff. I advised parents and encouraged them when students faltered. My life had daily purpose. I was a teacher. I felt like somebody. As we approached Christmas, my internship came to an end successfully completing my degree. I then followed my fiancé to another province where I knew no one. Suddenly I had no purpose because I no longer had a job. I felt lost and I floundered. I had never felt more lost in my life (turns out this would not be the last time). I was still the same person. What had changed? Everything that defined me for the past four months and even the few years before that was gone. I was not a teacher. I was an unemployed graduate living with a teaching certificate in a unfamiliar city. I thought, how could I feel so purposeless just because I did not have a job? The answer: I did not know who I was.

It would take me fifteen years to learn about Internal Values. When I learned about them, it kicked the door wide open on knowing who I was and my joy began to rise. For example, my top Internal Values are Connection, Comedy, Contribution.

**Connection:** I love engaging with people, having meaningful conversations, spending quality time with family and friends. (This value tells me I cannot sit in a cubicle for 30 years to crunch math numbers, but put me in a position where I can communicate, engage and encourage others, then I soar. This underlying value enables me to be a Human Resources Manager, a writer, an interviewer or a Life Coach. Finding ways to express connection in what I do makes me feel fulfilled.)

**Comedy:** I love having fun whether it is work or play. If I can laugh, even better. (This value tells me to stop doing activities that suck the life out of me and find more situations where fun is a factor or find ways to inject enjoyment into activities.)

**Contribution:** I love adding value whether it is making a difference in an organization or helping a friend that is struggling. (This value tells me I like being of service to others.)

Internal Values are a built-in guidance system that connects you to your Highest Self. Internal Values are the unique expression of your Highest Self. You could have two people who are Business Owners who love selling their product, but how they create their business outcomes is greatly dependent on what they value. One may love employing their values of **individualism, creativity** and **risk** to achieve their outcome while the other may need to embrace **collaboration, safety** and **security**. Both can create outcomes they want, but each are fulfilled in different ways on the journey. You are as unique as your values.

When you know your Internal Values, a shift happens because:

- you define yourself differently. You may be accustomed to defining yourself by conventional labels. Trade labels for values. You are not a mom of three with "X" job title. You are a fun loving, adventurous person who loves connecting with others OR a risk taker who is creative, spiritually directed and enjoys time by yourself in nature.

- your "being" (your set of Internal Values) informs your "doing". When you know who you are, you can choose activities, jobs, and spouses that align with who you are.

- knowing your Internal Values can be a springboard to help you find your purpose in life. When you define a framework of who you are, you have given yourself a starting point for your life to take shape.

To begin articulating your Internal Values, answer these questions:

What brings you joy?
What is a must have in your life?
What do you want more of in your life?
What's missing in your life?
Who are you being when you are at your best?

Record what values you identify. Next to the value, place a number beside it on a scale of 1 - 10 that rates how well you are honouring each value today.

| | |
|---|---|
| Creativity | 8 |
| Risk Taking | 5 |
| Connection | 7 |
| Freedom | 4 |
| Fun | 6 |

Recording a 10 means you are fully embracing and using that value today. Recording a 1 means you are not honouring the value at all. When you know your Internal Values, you can begin assessing how well you are honouring them. When you feel out of alignment, your joy may wane. Check in with yourself. You may not be living your life according to your values. If you say you must have connection with your family and you have not spent any quality time together, you may be feeling discontent. If you say you value creativity, but you have not been finding ways to express it, you may be feeling irritated. Pay attention to these feelings, they are pointing you somewhere. When you experience feelings of discontent or irritability, check in with how well you are honouring your values.

When you define yourself by your values, you begin to know what is non-negotiable in order for you to be joyous and fulfilled.

What do you value?

*"Deep contentment silences the pursuit of happiness."*

## Soul R$_x$ #79

## Trade Happiness for Fulfillment

A culture of pursuing happiness exists. If you ask people what they want in life, they will often say, "I just want to be happy." If you ask them what they want for their children. They will say, "I just want them to be happy." If you ask people to explain what "happy" is they are unsure how to explain it. The desire to be happy is everywhere, in the movies, in songs, and in commercials. It sets you up for failure when you believe happiness needs to be pursued and that it is out there somewhere.

Everyone knows what happiness feels like. Once you get a taste of it, you want more. It feels good. Who does not want to feel good? Happiness is like a drug, seductive, addictive, convincing you that a life well lived is a series of "happiness highs." You are lured to seek out your next happiness fix launching you in hot pursuit of happiness. To make it even tougher to find, you put parameters around it: you will be happy when you fall in love; you will be happy when you get the promotion; you will be happy when you lose the 25 pounds; you will be happy when you get out of debt. Happiness is not a future event. Happiness is an emotion that falls into the range of human emotions like anger, sadness, despair, or excitement. Happiness like all emotions are fleeting.

Searching for happiness can make you miserable. It makes people pine for what was, moments in time that cannot be relived, or it draws you into the illusion that you will rediscover happiness in the future. Somewhere along the way, the word happiness has become the catch all word to describe something that you are looking for, but have difficulty articulating.

What you really want is fulfillment, a deep contentment that silences the pursuit of happiness. You can have angry, sad or happy moments, but still have the overarching feeling of fulfillment in your life. Fulfillment is the foundation upon which you can build a life of meaning and significance. Leading a fulfilled life means you are living in alignment with your Highest Self. One of the best ways I know to feel fulfilled is to know what you value then live in alignment with those values. (See Soul $R_x$ #78: Know What You Value). When you live a life according to your values, you feel like you are living a life on purpose.

Fulfillment is sustainable and stable indicating a deep connection with self. Trade happiness for fulfillment.

What fulfills you?

*"Your Ego loves a label; your Highest Self does not need one."*

## Soul R$_x$ #80

## Refrain From Attaching Yourself To Labels

Go to any party or meeting, the conversation always turns to the simple question, "What do you do?" I was a stay at home mom for many years, so this question would make me anxious. I felt like a bit of an outsider not being a part of the "working world." I felt like the label "stay at home" mom was not enough. As soon as I became a Life Coach, however, I felt like I was holding onto a lifesaver. I had a shiny, new label that reduced the awkwardness in settings when I had to describe myself. All of a sudden, I was somebody too. How ridiculous! How could I feel better about myself by changing labels? The answer: I was looking outside of myself for definition rather than looking inside. I placed more importance on doing than being. If I had been comfortable with who I was being, the need to define myself would never have been an issue.

Labels, like job titles, can become substitutes for worthiness. Titles are great if I want to know what you do for a career, but it does not tell me anything about who you are. Attaching yourself to labels provides a false sense of security. What happens if you lose the title that you are so closely held to? Who are you without that title? Even the label "stay at home" mom only described what I was doing at a certain point in time. I am more than that and so are you.

Titles can generate safety. I know when people are really attached to titles because they tell you about it. They talk about it and convince you of how important they are. I feel empathy for them as the fall will be hard when that title goes away. The more closely held to a title, the greater the distance from your Highest Self.

When you strip away the title, answering the question, "Who Am I?" can be overwhelming. Your outer labels will change, but your Essence will remain the same. If you search for a label to define you, you will always be searching for who you are as labels change because jobs and life roles change, but the ultimate YOU does not change. Finding fulfillment based on an outwardly changing world is stressful. It robs you of your joy if you do not know who you are. The greater pleasure you derive from a label, the more difficult it will be when the label changes. Your Ego loves a label; your Highest Self does not need one.

Who are you without your labels?

*"The process of becoming who you want to be is a practice."*

## Soul R<sub>x</sub> #81

## *Practice Yourself Into Being*

In the sports world, practice is necessary for the constant movement toward mastery. Sports provide endless opportunity for growth. In order to be an Olympic athlete, constant practice is necessary to play at this esteemed level. Even though there are setbacks, athletes continue to show up and practice to become their best.

A few years ago I learned to play hockey, an activity that proved to have a lot of comic therapy. I didn't play sports growing up, so I had no athletic experience on which to rely. Luckily, I was able to join a new team where everyone was mostly at the same skill level. Zero. This was the team for me. Because most of us did not know how to play hockey, our first year was dedicated to learning the game. For one hour every week, our coach, taught us new skills. Our learning formula: Practice. Fail. Repeat. Learning the new skills was challenging, but we continued to show up each week. Little by little we improved although there was a lot of falling, laughing, great attempts, epic fails, and a few injuries. We began the season as chicks with sticks, but by the end of the season, we were hockey players. We became hockey players because we practiced being hockey players.

Your "beingness" requires the same level of dedication. If you want more of something in your life, show up consistently and practice that which you want to become.

If you want to be a more grateful person, practice gratitude.
If you want to be more in the moment, practice presence.

If you want to be a more helpful person, practice helping.
If you want to be more compassionate, practice compassion.

The process of becoming who you want to be is a practice. Who do you want to be? Truly. Start acting the way you want to show up. Becoming is conscious work. If you are very practiced at showing up one way, it will take effort to show up in a new way. This is not about becoming something you are not. It is about coming closer to your Highest Self, achieving true authenticity.

Start practicing who you want to be. Keep showing up. There is a sense of pure joy and fulfillment when you are moving through life as the person you know you can be.

What do you feel compelled to practice to become the person you want to be?

*"You are a co-creator of a beautiful of life."*

## Soul R$_x$ #82

## *Develop A Spiritual Practice*

A spiritual practice is a highly aware activity that strengthens the connection with your Highest Self. Practices allow you to tap into the part of you that you sense is there, but cannot see. Growing up, I had practices and traditions thrust upon me. Saying my prayers before bed was a practice. I would kneel by my bedside to recite three prayers: Our Father, Hail Mary, and Glory Be. I had no idea why I was reciting these other than this is what Catholics did. It did not make sense. I did not feel better for having recited them. It only made me feel guilty if I forgot. Those prayers fell away because it did not feel purposeful, but I had a longing in my heart for a connection with something larger than myself. As I grew older, I slowly returned to prayer, but it sounded more like a conversation. It was my voice, my words. As I grew older still, I was able to strengthen the connection to my Highest Self through the act of writing. Writing has now become my dominant spiritual practice. Not something that I have to do, but something that I want to do. Writing has become a beautiful act. When I write to my Highest Self, my Highest Self writes back.

There are many ways to bring yourself into connection with your Highest Self. Those spiritual practices include:

- Praying. Open up the communication lines between you and your Highest Self.
- Practicing yoga. It is more than exercise. It is a placeholder for the present moment.

- Expressing gratitude.
- Reading literature that inspires you.
- Writing to create an exchange between you and your Highest Self.
- Connecting with nature.
- Any activity that involves the arts…. painting, sculpting, woodworking, acting.
- Meditating
- Journaling
- Practicing creativity.

Developing a spiritual practice is recognizing you are a spiritual being having a human experience. As you strengthen the connection with your Highest Self, you view life differently. A beautiful life unfolds as a result of the amazing connection with your Inner Being. When you make a conscious effort to be positive, patient, joy filled, creative, and peaceful, you are allowing your Highest Self to work through you. You get to be a co-creator of a beautiful life.

What spiritual practice would help deepen the connection with your Inner Self?

*"Vulnerability is not synonymous with weakness;
it is a testament to strength."*

## Soul R<sub>x</sub> #83

## Be Vulnerable

Vulnerability is the channel through which your Authentic Self is birthed. You get to authenticity through vulnerability. One of the first times I remember my vulnerability being addressed was when I attended my first coaching course. There were twenty six strangers sitting in a circle in a conference room deep in the belly of a hotel. I was asked to come into the circle to be coached by one of the leaders. Baring my Soul was not what I wanted to do. I began joking around and making wise cracks to avoid giving the real answer to the posed questions. Very quickly the experienced Coach drew attention to the fact that I was using comedy as a defence mechanism. She was onto me. I felt exposed. Comedy is what I employ to deflect unwanted attention away from me or to prevent being hurt.

When you act and feel like a fake, authenticity stays at a distance preventing you from real, authentic connections with others and most importantly with yourself. When the Coach asked me to drop the comedic routine, I learned things about myself. The Coach was able to churn up answers from deep within me like waves churning up treasures from the ocean floor. If you want to have deep, rich relationships, beginning with yourself, authenticity needs to be present.

Vulnerability is not synonymous with weakness; it is a testament to strength. People who are internally strong and confident know that being vulnerable is a way of connecting deeply with yourself and with others. I had the pleasure of connecting with a passionate Soul who was encountering a difficult business situation. She was honest and upfront about her current state. She did not put on a façade because she did not have time for pretending. Her vulnerability helped build trust quickly in our new relationship which increased my desire to want to help her more. If people question your authenticity, they are not quick to trust, connect or help.

Being vulnerable can make you feel naked and raw. People see through to your Soul. There are risks associated with vulnerability. The girl may not say yes to you asking her out on a date. Your first art project may not be a success. You may not get the job. There are risks to revealing who you are and what you want. As you practice vulnerability, however, you become more comfortable with authenticity. The risks of being vulnerable diminish as you claim who you are. Drop the mask. Keep it real. Embrace who you are. Show the world who you are. Move closer to your Authentic Self.

When is it difficult for you to be vulnerable?

*"When you listen and act based on your own internal guidance,
you place value on you."*

## Soul R$_x$ #84

## *Make Decisions With Your Internal Committee*

Years ago I worked in an office where it was decided the office was going to be redecorated. One person was assigned to lead the project. It was not long before others in the office offered up their thoughts on how it should be decorated. We soon realized that we were not going to get a consensus. Everyone had a different idea about how it should look depending on what they liked. We were not going to be able to decorate by committee.

Running your life is the same way. You cannot run your life by external committee. People's opinions are based on their experiences, beliefs and values. When you ask others for their opinions, you are placing more value on what others think rather than what you think. Seeking external guidance is a way for you to gain acceptance and approval of others which is fear based. You fear what others will think of your decisions. You fear you will disappoint others, but other people do not get to live your life, you do. You get to live with the rewards and the consequences.

You have access to a great internal committee on which to base your life. You can make decisions based on what your gut is telling you, what you value, where your emotional compass is pointing you, and your previous experience. You have a wealth of information residing within you. When you live according to your internal guidance, you will make decisions based on what you truly want even if you make decisions that may not be popular with others. When you listen and act based on your own internal guidance, you place value on you. What you want matters.

When you have the courage to lead your own life rather than ask everyone around you what they think, you have connected with your Highest Self. You are living from a place of trust. Trust that you are making the best decisions for you. When you do not take a national poll every time you make a decision, it shows you are taking 100% responsibility for your life. This is a powerful way to live.

What is your internal committee guiding you to do?

*"Living a life of purpose is living a life on purpose."*

## Soul R$_x$ #85

## *Bring Purpose To Your Life*

Your life becomes purposeful when you bring purpose to it. I live in a two storey home. Often the dining room went unused relegated to being a space that housed unused furniture, an extra place to dry clothes or to entertain relatives for the handful of big holiday celebrations. I decided that if I was going to have the space, it was going to be purposeful. What's the point of having it if you are not going to use it? Now we make an effort to have dinner in our dining room as a family on any random day of the week. That day is special because we say it is and we make it so. To make it special, we remove ourselves from the visual clutter of the aftermath of preparing a meal in the kitchen. We light candles and dim the chandelier as if we were in a restaurant. It sets a different tone for conversation and connection with each other. It has purpose now because we gave it one.

There was a time when our family did not use the living room either because it was not inviting. A new paint colour, a fireplace and new furniture brought it to life. It has since become a space of creativity and connection. It is where I read and write and our children play piano and do crafts. My husband and I talk about life and business over a cup of coffee on a Sunday morning. The living room, once purposeless, is now a retreat from the other noisy spaces in the house. Spaces in your home become purposeful when you bring purpose to them. As you shift rooms, you shift purpose. The same is true of your life.

When you hold to the belief that you only have one purpose in life, it can create anxiety and disconnection. Too often people spend their whole life searching for that one BIG thing hoping to make sense of their life. The truth is you have two purposes: an internal purpose and an external purpose. You may have many external purposes in life. You may be a mother, a charity volunteer, or a valuable member at work. Your purpose might be to express your creativity in song writing or be creative in business. Your life is purposeful and your purpose changes depending on the activity or circumstance that brings you delight. The pleasure you receive from your external purpose is very much driven by what you value (See Soul $R_x$ #78). When you live in alignment with your values, you feel fulfilled. You feel like you are living a life on purpose.

Your internal purpose is to align with your Highest Self. This is your most important and meaningful purpose. To align with your Highest Self is to be enlightened and awakened. It is to be fully aware that you are detached from your Ego at that moment. When you are detached from Ego, you are immersed in presence. Presence allows quality of life to show up. You no longer go through the daily routines of life absentmindedly. You drop off the kids at daycare being fully present for them instead of already being at your 9 o'clock meeting. Enjoyment comes from mundane tasks when your mind is not racing to take you to another time and place. Your internal purpose of enlightenment is a gift.

Although your external purposes may be different from others, you are united with everyone through your internal purpose. Living a life *of* purpose is living a life *on* purpose.

How does knowing you have an internal and an external life purpose impact you?

# CELEBRATION

*"Gratitude is an easy point of entry into a spiritual practice."*

## Soul R$_x$ #86

## *Bookend Your Day With Thanks*

If you have been looking for an easy point of entry into a spiritual practice, gratitude is a great beginning. When you open your eyes each morning and when you close them at night, say thank you. Thank you is the simplest prayer.

Gratitude serves many purposes:

- Expressing gratitude moves you to the present moment bringing you to a state of awareness that says "I am paying attention right now." As you move through your day, it can be difficult to hold onto that awareness, but regardless of what transpires, expressions of gratitude before you go to sleep will return you to peace at night. By giving thanks, you align with your Highest Self and separate yourself temporarily from your Ego. Continue giving thanks throughout your day to return to the present moment.

- Gratitude also serves to change the way you look at your life. What you focus on expands. If you focus on the negative, you create negative momentum. Think about when you have experienced a negative situation. The more you thought about it, talked about it with someone else, complained about it, the situation seemed to grow. Negativity can take deep root, but the same can be true of focusing on the positive, thereby, creating positive momentum. Activating gratitude is the catalyst for positive momentum. Gratitude makes you feel good.

- Developing a habit of giving thanks when times are good will make it easier to be grateful when times are not. How can you become more grateful? Train yourself to look at life through the lens of gratitude. Gratitude is a perspective. Imagine putting on a pair of "gratitude glasses." What do you choose to see? Train yourself to see the good things in your life.

A gratitude practice is applicable everywhere in your life. Gratefulness can be found in successes. "I am grateful for getting the promotion or I am grateful for achieving my goals." Gratitude can also be found in the lining of defeats. You may not have gotten the job, but you are grateful for the experience gained from the process. Your relationship may not have worked out, but you are grateful because now you know what you do not want. Gratitude also fine tunes your ability to see the simple things that can be overlooked like a morning songbird that rejoices outside your window.

Gratitude is a practice that you can develop until it becomes a part of you. Practice finding things to be grateful for in all situations and watch what happens in your life.

What are you grateful for?

*"Embrace unpredictability. It may not always be that way."*

## Soul R$_x$ #87

## *Enjoy Where You Are Right Now*

Life is cyclical. It is only natural that you will experience low points and high points in your life. Often it is just one part of your life that you may be struggling with, but you tend to turn your back on everything else to give your undivided attention to that one thing that is troubling you; for example, if you are pining over when you will meet the love of your life, you will become so focused on that aspect, it will consume all of your attention that you forget to enjoy the other aspects of your life such as recognizing you have a great place to work or that you have amazing friends or you can take care of yourself financially or that you are great at helping others. Sometimes the one thing in your life that you are not happy about can overshadow everything else that is amazing. Do not allow that one thing that is troubling you to separate you from what is working well.

Here is a love e-mail from a mother to her daughter to help quiet her daughter's concerns about finding the love of her life in her 20's:

*Subject: Enjoy the excitement of not knowing*

Being in yours twenties can be unsettling, but if I could go back in time to advise my twenty-five year old self, I would say-- enjoy the excitement of not knowing; not knowing which career you will end up with, not knowing who your life partner will be, not knowing how many children you will have, etc. Know there is so much to look forward to. Some day you will be working at your dream career until you are 55 or 60, your three grown kids off at college and your husband at the golf course. You will be comfortable, peaceful and be able to say, "Remember the exciting years of being twenty?" instead of remembering your twenties as frightful years like most people do. Enjoy each day, my pretty, and know how valuable you are to Earth and to everyone. And know that everything works out, not without challenges, but it does work out. Be yourself and you will have everything you work for and dream of.

Love Mommy.

This daughter's worry over not finding the love of her life in her twenties overshadowed every other part of her life making her twenties less enjoyable. This loving mom got it right. Enjoy where you are right now. Embrace unpredictability. It may not always be that way. Refocus your energy on what is good about your life. The rest will come.

What is good about where you are right now in your life?

*"Anyone who knows their true self worth would not willingly betray themselves."*

## Soul R<sub>x</sub> #88

## Honour Yourself

The greatest relationship you have is the one you have with yourself. Honouring yourself is knowing that you are worthy. Anyone who knows their true self worth would not willingly betray themselves. The ultimate betrayal is when you do not honour yourself. Ways you tend to betray yourself:

- when your gut tells you "no" and you proceed anyway
- when you know you should eat better and do not
- when you should have spoken up and did not
- when you spend money you do not have
- when you know you are in the wrong relationship and stay
- when you tolerate people treating you in an unkind way
- when you do not speak the truth
- when you do not show up as your best self
- when you choose to ignore your dreams and callings
- when you give your power away
- when you know who you are and do not live the life you desire

Dishonouring yourself is not knowing your self worth. Know you are worthy of all the wonderful things that life has to offer you. Know who you are. Dig, provoke, interrogate, examine, question, challenge and enrich the relationship with yourself. Decide what you want. It is not a final decision. You can change your mind. When you make the choice to honour yourself on more days than not, you are moving in alignment with your Highest Self.

The benefits of honouring yourself:

- increased confidence
- boosted self-image
- new found self-esteem
- a deep knowing that you are on your path
- a general sense of feeling good
- you think differently choosing to pay attention to the good thoughts versus the debilitating thoughts
- pride in standing up for yourself
- knowing you are courageous

How can you honour yourself today?

*"Feeling good is good self-care."*

## Soul R<sub>x</sub> #89

## *Do Things That Make You Feel Good*

Life is meant to be enjoyed. Stop doing things that you feel you should do. Stop doing things that make you sad or angry, or just plain suck the life out of you. For every Soul sucking thing you do, there are an equal number of amazing things you could be doing. Do things that make you feel good. Partake in activities that light you up. Not sure what lights you up? Date life. Just like when you are finding a mate, you date different people. Try different activities or groups. Make a point to find what brings you joy.

You can become very practiced at doing things that do not make you feel good. Things that you do not enjoy have a way of sneaking into your life. You take on one activity then another. If you have ever driven a car on a well travelled road, you can feel the grooves of the road where thousands of cars have driven. With just a little guidance by the driver, the car can easily stay on the road by following the grooves. Life can get like this. With just a little guidance, it can plod along without much excitement. To move off the well worn roadway, you need two hands on the wheel to direct the car onto a new path. You have the same power with your life. Feeling good means staying conscious in your life. Find the paths that make you feel good.

Life is not always made up of joyful activities. There are certain things in life you have to do, even though you may not enjoy them as much such as making kids' school lunches, cleaning out the cat litter, mowing the lawn, but that only takes up a small amount of time. Do not make something out to be bigger than it is. Stop assuming things take more time than they do. I had a friend who always procrastinated emptying the dishwasher because it was a time consuming task. One day she decided to time how long it took to empty the dishwasher. She realized it actually only took two minutes. Emptying the dishwasher became less of an onerous task when she knew it was only going to take a short time. You actually have more time than you think to pursue activities that fill you up. Be effective with your time and start to do more of what makes you feel good.

Feeling good is good self-care.

How can you begin to feel good more often?

*"Rituals give you a greater appreciation for the ordinary."*

## Soul R$_x$ #90

## *Transform Routine Into Ritual*

Your days are filled with routines which serve a purpose. Routines help you move easily through many parts of your day without having to think about mundane activities such as getting ready for work, driving to work, workday beginnings, or getting kids out the door in the morning. Routines can also help build habits which set you up for success. If you want to work out regularly in the morning, you may establish a routine such as setting out your workout clothes the night before, having a water bottle filled in the fridge, having your music ready to go and setting an alarm that gets you up early. Routines are very helpful to guide you through your day.

A routine is different from a ritual, however. Routines are completed with a dull awareness requiring little attention to move through an activity. Routines are transformed into rituals when you bring awareness to the activity. A ritual is a practice that brings you in union with your Highest Self. It is a practice of bringing awareness to your activities allowing you to forge an alliance with the present moment.

The act of getting out of bed in the morning is routine, but breathing in the dawn with your attention is ritual. Taking a shower is routine. Feeling the warmth of the water cascading over your shoulders is a ritual. Making coffee in the morning is a routine. Listening to the sound of coffee pouring into your cup, enjoying the smell and feeling how the warm cup in your hand makes you feel are rituals. An awakening happens when you bring attention to the mundane.

A ritual is a way of bringing meaning into your life through the smallest of moments. Rituals create the effect of slowing time down allowing you to experience depth in your life. Rituals give you a greater appreciation for the ordinary. They make everyday important.

What routines could you transform into rituals?

*"Do not miss the ordinary while seeking extraordinary."*

## *Soul R$_x$ #91*

## *Celebrate Ordinary*

Life is mostly made up of ordinary moments: a warm wind on your face, biting into a juicy fresh picked strawberry, the warmth of a hug, the dizziness of a first kiss, eating cereal at the kitchen table in your pyjamas, sunshine through a window or the stillness of your pet outstretched in its bed taking a nap. Ordinary has depth and richness if you take the time to feel it, touch it, taste it, smell it, see it. To experience the richness of ordinary requires presence.

In University, I enrolled in a drama course. As my drama teacher crawled around on her knees on the cold classroom floor demonstrating a scene, she asked us "to slow the action down" in the scene we were about to enact. She not only wanted us to "do" the scene by merely reading the lines, but she wanted us to "be" in the scene. She wanted us to explore all that the scene had to offer. She wanted us to experience the emotions of the characters and to capitalize on the interactions between people experiencing the words that were exchanged. She did not want us to miss the opportunity of what each moment had to offer. We soon realized that there was more to the moment than just saying our lines. I could either just deliver the seemingly ordinary lines on the page to get them said or I could be in tune with what was happening within the scene. I watched the responses of the other characters as they reacted to what I had to say. Did it upset them or make them happy? To "be" in the scene forces you to pay attention. It forces you to "slow the action down."

Life is a series of ordinary moments wedged in between the fewer extraordinary ones. You can dismiss them or celebrate them. Celebrating ordinary is a choice to "be" in the scenes of your life. Slow the action down. Experience the depth and richness of life. Do not miss ordinary while seeking extraordinary.

Ordinary has something to offer you.

What would you gain by experiencing life in slow motion?

*POWER*

*"You are only defeated if you think you are."*

## Soul R$_x$ #92

## *Learn To Take The Losses Without Getting Defeated*

One evening I was watching a documentary about a major league baseball player who was trying to stay in the major leagues. It was an emotional roller coaster ride because his career was on the line. Ultimately, he was able to extend his career by perfecting his knuckleball pitch. He made a powerful statement about his career in baseball. You need to learn to take the losses without getting defeated. Anyone working toward a goal needs to remind themselves of this statement as it underscores the importance of mindset. You are only defeated if you think you are.

On the road to success, there will always be setbacks, small and large. It is a given. A big part of moving through the defeats or temporary losses is how you deal with them. Sports is a great teacher of life lessons. Recently I learned how to play golf. I noticed that if I focused on any bad shots, my resident Inner Critic would pop its head out like a bird in a cuckoo clock to start a firestorm of negative thoughts such as: "You are never going to be able to play this game." "You started too late to learn it well." If I allow my Inner Critic to feed me negative thoughts of defeat, I am not going to have fun which will negatively impact my game. My other option when I make a bad shot is to quickly shift my focus from negative thinking to what I am doing well or what I am enjoying about the game. The fun factor rises when I enjoy activities. My emotional state is directly related to my desire to continue playing the game. My desire to play the game greatly affects the outcome.

Life is like sports. How you view losses will determine the likelihood of being in a stuck or defeated mindset. A loss is only a setback if it is viewed as such. Reframe your perspective on defeat.

How can you effectively deal with setbacks?

*"Choose to live with the cheerleader, not the critic."*

## Soul R<sub>x</sub> #93

## Develop An Inner Coach

Why is it so much easier to be kind to others and to encourage them, but not extend the same compassion to yourself? Develop a voice so loud inside your head that all you can hear is enthusiasm being belted out of a megaphone reminding you that you are awesome, that you possess the necessary skills and talents, that you have stamina, are competent and capable, have lots to offer, and are of value. Choose to live with the cheerleader, not the critic.

The greatest gift I can give to people as a Coach is my gift of encouragement. It is amazing to watch people jolt to life as if you have just given them CPR. It is like they are starved for validation. Your worthiness can be depleted by the Inner Critic. Spend less time taming the Inner Critic and more time firing up your Inner Coach. When you crank up the volume on your Inner Coach, you will not be able to hear your Inner Critic.

Name your Inner Coach. Write down encouraging statements that you want your Inner Coach to say to you. Give yourself encouragement often. Call forth your Inner Coach when you need inspiration, assurance and strength. Employing your Inner Coach aligns you with your Highest Self.

What is your Inner Coach's name?

# Name Your Inner Coach

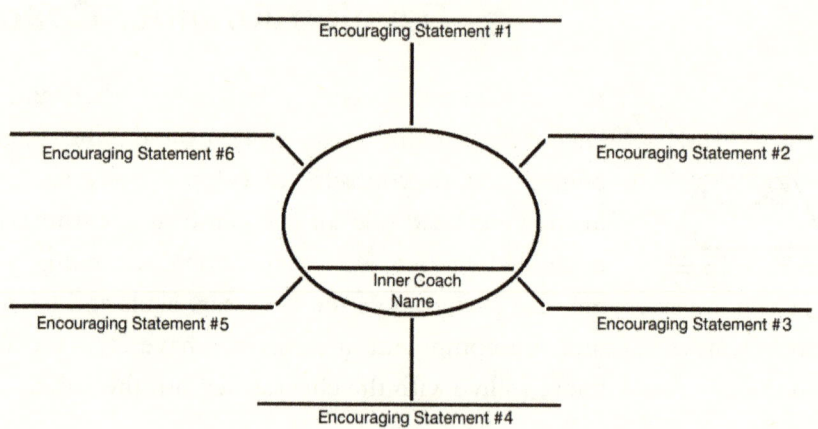

*"Impatience is a momentary disconnection from your Highest Self."*

## Soul R<sub>x</sub> #94

## Become Patient

Practicing patience shows you are interested in a high quality inner life. If you are an impatient person, there must be a purposeful, internal shift to become patient. Becoming patient is a practice. It requires awareness around triggers that launch impatience. It requires a commitment to your inner peace. Being patient moves you into alignment with your Highest Self where peace is found. When you are tired of the internal turmoil, commit yourself to patience. Spend more time with your Highest Self.

When you align with your Highest Self, you are stepping into trust. Patience is trust. When you are impatient with a situation wanting it to happen faster than it is, you are not trusting that things are working out for you. What you resist, persists. Obsessing about the outcome causes greater resistance. Resisting less is trusting more.

Think of a time when you have been in a grocery store line up becoming impatient. You become obsessed with the outcome: getting out of the grocery store as fast as you can. You start examining the length of the lines wondering if there is a shorter line to which you can move. Sure enough you are lured away from your line that is at a standstill moving to the shortest line you can find. No sooner do you jump into that line then it stops moving because of a price check. All of a sudden, the line you were in starts moving. Frustration sets in. Your impatience has cost you your peace.

How many times have you become impatient while driving? You pass a slower car in front of you, speeding past the car feeling frustrated, mumbling words under your breath while glaring at the passing driver only to get to a stop light, look in your rear view mirror to find the person you passed right behind you, happy as can be bobbing their head to music. You did not save any time. The only thing you left behind when you blew past the slower driver was your peace. The momentary frustration did not save you time. If anything, it could have put you at risk for an accident and it definitely stole your peace.

Moments like these are temporary disconnections from your Highest Self. Impatience causes internal turmoil. When you are tired of not feeling good, when you are tired of giving up your peace, become patient. The practice of becoming a patient person is the practice of being aligned with your Highest Self.

What makes you impatient?

*"Worry walks you away from peace."*

## Soul R$_x$ #95

## *Minimize Worrying*

When my mother started to lose her speech and mobility, for unknown reasons, worry ran unchecked in my head. Every frightening scenario played out in my mind. As she was tested for each disease, I waited for the results holding my breath wondering if this would be the diagnosis that would change our family's trajectory. After a couple of years, she got a diagnosis of Degenerative Cerebellum (maybe). This diagnosis did not fit into my worry spectrum. I spent a year and a half worrying about other diseases that were more common. I allowed myself to tell stories that frightened me.

There is a lot of lost sleep, lack of joy, and dullness in your life when worry slips behind the wheel. The biggest lesson I learned going through this experience is most of what you worry about never comes true. Worry places you in a negative holding pattern. More importantly, worry knocks you out of alignment with your Highest Self causing much unneeded mental torture.

To minimize worrying:

- Do not give unneeded attention to an unwanted situation. More focus only means more power.
- Stop inventing outcomes that have not yet happened.
- Shut down scary thoughts and shift to good thoughts about the situation.
- Focus on possibility.

- Focus on what you want.
- Take time out to connect with yourself.
- Breathe deeply and follow where your breath takes you. Allow it to walk you back to peace.

Take control of your thoughts. Worry walks you away from peace. Stay connected to your Highest Self even in the most difficult times. This is where your peace is found. It is this connection and alignment that will keep you sane, comforted and keep worry at bay.

When worry comes knocking, what will be your action plan?

*"As a child, words gave birth to your power."*

## Soul R$_x$ #96

## *Words Matter*

As a child, words gave birth to your power. As you identified objects and people in your environment, you became powerful because you could articulate what you wanted. Words gave you the power to be understood. As you began to move in this world, words took on even more power. Every single minute of the day you tell the world who you are through what you say and how you say it. Words have energy and force when expressed with tone, intention, energy, emphasis and attitude.

Your choice of words reveal where you are on your spiritual journey. When you are using your words to lift people up, you are in sync with your Highest Self. When you are using words to strike others down you are walking hand in hand with your Ego. Your choice of words either moves you toward your Highest Self or away from it. Simply, your spiritual journey, the distance you have to travel to find peace, is shortened when you become conscious of the energy you are putting out into the world.

Choose your words carefully as they can be used to:

- strike people down
- lift people up
- participate in drama or gossip
- be used as a weapon
- inspire
- betray others

- betray yourself
- heal
- mend
- voice gratitude
- create art
- challenge people
- encourage others

Words matter. Words are powerful.

To what will you lend your words?

*"You are in nature and nature is in you."*

## Soul R$_x$ #97

## *Use Mother Nature To Heal You*

Mother Nature reminds you of your power by showing you her own. You are in nature and nature is in you. Mother Nature is powerful, calm, cheerful, harmonious, fun, entertaining, quiet, diverse, restorative, thrilling, colourful, peaceful, fierce and so much more. She reveals her power in many ways:

- ocean surf roars
- waves lull
- birds serenade
- trees whisper
- clouds dance
- grass is
- animals frolic
- wind swirls
- air refreshes
- a night sky entertains
- earth grounds you

Nature quietly reflects back to you what you need to know. It shows that you can live in peace, yet sometimes be fierce. It shows you that life is meant to be lived vibrantly, yet blending in is sometimes needed. There is a time for working hard, yet there is room for rest and renewal. There is always time for play. The messages she sends are plentiful. What message is for you?

Nature is a remedy. Have you ever just needed to go outside to get some air? You may be escaping from a situation, but amazed at how the air brushing on your face calms you down or how a walk in the woods brings you back to the present moment or how sitting on a beach with the sand between your toes listening to the ocean surf makes you grateful. Your senses pick up the signals of what Mother Nature is transmitting. Nature sends her healing power through sight, touch, taste, hearing, and smell. What natural surroundings are good for your Soul? The ocean? The mountains? The forest? What do these environments do for you? What smells appeal to you? What images can you never get enough of? Use nature to repair yourself.

Start paying attention to your surroundings. A reconnection with nature is a Soul connection. Nature takes you back to your resting place where you Highest Self always resides.

How does nature heal you?

*"Air is to your lungs as laughter is to your Soul; it just fills you up."*

## Soul R$_x$ #98

## *Develop A Sense Of Humour*

One of the best compliments I have ever received came from a friend who said, "If you want to find Dana in a room, follow the laughter." That statement sums up who I am. I love to laugh and have fun. I have a natural ability to see the funny in things. Perhaps a little too much funny sometimes. I can credit my parents for my sense of humour. My mother is organically funny. She does not always realize she is being funny. My father is purposely humorous finding the funny nugget in most situations. Both my parents express their sense of humour through storytelling. I too enjoy telling stories from a funny perspective. Having a sense of humour brings light into the world. It has a double impact of making you and others feel good.

Develop your sense of humour by using humour as a perspective. Practice seeing the funny in things. When I tell stories about my life, I purposely craft them as funny because I see situations as funny. I am self-deprecating; I laugh at myself. Like my dad, I look for the funny nugget. Life is not that serious.

Developing a sense of humour serves your spiritual growth:

- Humour allows you to temporarily detach from your Ego. You drop your inhibitions when you are willing to laugh at yourself. People want to feel good and they want to connect with people that make them feel good. Humour enables that.

- There is an old saying that "Laughter is the best medicine." When laughter strikes, you cannot think of anything else. Laughter fully engages you in the present moment where you unknowingly dance with your Highest Self.

Air is to your lungs as laughter is to your Soul; it just fills you up.

What can you do to develop a sense of humour?

*"An excuse is another way to say NO to life."*

## *Soul R<sub>x</sub> #99*

## *Remove the Excuses*

An excuse is another way to say "NO" to life. No to getting fit, no to a relationship, no to stretching yourself, no to building a business, no to success, no to love, no to growth. Whatever your excuse is, what is causing you to say "NO" to life?

Saying no to life generally falls under two main categories:

### Fear

Fear fuels the excuses. There is fear of not being liked, fear of being vulnerable, fear of failing, fear of being hurt, fear of looking stupid, fear of being seen, fear of being seen in your stretchy workout pants, fear of disappointment, fear of rejection, or fear of being wrong. "Fear" and "NO" are like two gangsters walking with swagger through the neighbourhood terrifying everyone. They scare people away from the juicy, richness of life - the fit body, the business you wanted to start, a great relationship, a deep friendship. Fear creates uncertainty disabling you from beginning. It kills all desire to accomplish goals even if, when accomplished, they would bring you great fulfillment.

### Lack of Effort

You want the outcome and all the glory that comes with accomplishing goals, but you do not want to do the work. Lack of effort causes you to miss out on the fun of a book launch, the compliments that are bestowed on you when you achieve the goal of a fit body, the money that your business brings, or the recognition of leading an important project. In order to get the outcome, you have to begin and finish. Only effort brings you glory. You cannot determine what the outcome will be without starting something. Lack of effort can be fuelled by the uncertainty of an outcome. You may achieve your goal or not, but whatever the outcome, it will be so much richer when you show up in life and do the work. Are you willing to invest your time without knowing the outcome?

Effort brings new people, ideas, wisdom and success into your life. Even if your desired outcome is not what you had originally envisioned, you took the journey. It is in the journey where the juiciness lies. You find out who you are. You will not regret giving your best. When you entertain excuses, you are not aligned with your Highest Self. When you are not aligned with your Highest Self, you are never quite satisfied with life. You know there is something more *and* you are frustrated that you cannot get your hands on it. The only thing keeping you from getting your hands on it is yourself. You have to break up the gangsters "Fear" and "No." Be willing to be vulnerable and start saying "yes." Say yes to life, say yes to you and say yes to your Highest Self. The next time you find yourself making an excuse for something you really want to do, think about saying "yes" and see what happens.

Success is closer than you think. When you are willing to minimize the fear and do the work, success shows up gradually then suddenly.

What would saying yes more often do for your life?

*"Decisions allow you to lead an empowered life."*

## *Soul R$_x$ #100*

## *Make A Decision*

Being decisive is one of the most empowering ways to move through life. It does not matter that your decisions always create the best outcomes, it matters that you are able to decide. Decision making is a practiced way of being. The more you decide, the better you get at making decisions. Decisiveness makes you stronger. When you become a decision maker in your life you are taking responsibility for you. Every decision takes you somewhere. Some decisions will take you closer to where you want to be, others will take you away from it. Get experienced with making decisions and living with the outcomes.

Indecision is tiring. You wander around in circles never creating any movement forward. You mentally exhaust yourself. To make a decision is to take back your power.

**Decisions** are POWERFUL mental shifts because they can be life changing. They have the power to change the trajectory of your life.

When you decide not to be broke anymore. **Powerful.**
When you decide not to take the abuse anymore. **Powerful.**
When you decide to stand up for yourself. **Powerful.**
When you decide to remove yourself from drama. **Powerful.**
When you decide to love yourself. **Powerful.**
When you decide not to believe the negative stories you tell yourself. **Powerful.**
When you decide not to believe other people's negative stories about yourself. **Powerful.**

When you decide to live your life on purpose. **Powerful.**
When you decide to live from a space of compassion. **Powerful.**
When you decide to be an encourager. **Powerful.**
When you decide to take responsibility for your life. **Powerful.**

Nothing is more empowering than taking control of your own life and creating the life you desire.

**Decisions** build confidence. Decision making is like building a muscle. The more decisions you make, the more practiced and stronger you will become at it. It feels good to be decisive.

**Decisions** allow you to create your own personal policies which proactively guide you through life. Decide in advance how you want to behave. When the challenges come, you will already know your response.

If someone cuts you off in traffic, how will you behave?
If someone challenges you, how will you react?
When someone upsets you, how will you behave?
When you feel anger rising, how will you handle it?
When you witness bullying, how will you respond?

**Decisions** make struggles easier. Life becomes easier when you decide what you want; for example, if you are conscious of what you are choosing to eat and then are invited to a party, you make decisions around how to effectively manage your food choices. Perhaps you decide to eat before the party or decide you will only eat certain foods at the party.

When you get asked to volunteer for the umpteenth time, it is easier to say no if you have already decided where you will volunteer your time. "No thank you, I have already made other commitments." The beauty of decision making is you no longer have to think about what you will do. Deciding in advance allows you to execute according to plan. Decisions remove struggles from everyday life.

What decisions do you need to make to live a more empowered life?

*"Assumptions force you to play in the dark rather than in the light."*

## *Soul R$_x$ #101*

## *Assume Nothing*

 Assumptions are the fine details you tend to use as fillers to round out a story. You imagine what the other person said or felt or you make predictions about what you think will happen. The problem with this thinking is that you often begin to believe it is the truth and then begin reacting to the new story you invented versus the actual situation that has unfolded.

Assumptions also make you avoid having important conversations because you have already played out how it is going to go. "I will say this and then she is going to say this and then we will get nowhere so there is no point in having the conversation at all." Making assumptions will scare you from showing up to have real conversations and solving real problems.

How have you reacted to another based on your assumptions:

- purposefully not talked to someone?
- ignored someone?
- withheld a Like on their Social Media post?
- judged them?
- not have been nice to another?
- talked about the other person?

Assumptions prevent you from dealing in truth. Deal with what is, not what you think is. Your invented stories cause pain. You are better than that. Become aware of when you make assumptions. Are there certain people that trigger your assumptive storytelling?

Assumptions disconnect you from Highest Self. When you assume, you are playing in the dark rather than in the light. When you walk away from assumptions, you walk toward your Highest Self.

Who are you being when you make assumptions?

# *BONUS*
## *SOUL PRESCRIPTIONS*

*"Every challenged fear is an opportunity for an awakening."*

## Soul R<sub>x</sub> #102

## *Face Your Fears*

Fears are like weeds in a garden. Left unchecked, they invade, choking the growth of the vegetables. Like weeds, fear will choke out all that you want and everything you were meant to be. Face your fears to get the life you want.

Fear shows up in many ways:

- discomfort
- jealousy
- hate
- pettiness
- inauthenticity
- feeling stuck
- perfectionism

Fear shows up because:

- you want things to be predictable and you want to know the outcome.
- you want your own way.
- you do not want to be judged.
- you want to be liked.
- you want to get ahead of another.
- you want to be successful.
- you want something immensely.

Change your perspective on fear as it is a great teacher. Fear can show you what you want. The bigger the fear, the bigger the want. Fear pops up when you want to ask someone on a date, tackle a new ski hill, launch a company or play music in front of a live audience for the first time. The more scared you feel, the greater the indication that it is something you want. When you push through it, you will be better regardless of the outcome. Have no regrets. Do not ignore your fears; pay attention to them. Are they pointing you to what you want?

Fear moves you closer to your goals. Every challenged fear is an opportunity for an awakening. What your fears give you is greater than what they take from you. Every time you conquer a fear, you take a step in the right direction. Push through fears even if you have unsuccessful outcomes. You can easily get discouraged thinking that the action was not worth it, but instead look at the result. What did you learn? Where has this experience taken you? Praise yourself for challenging the fear. You are always one step closer to success when you push past fear.

Fears push you toward authenticity. Fear is a nudge from your Highest Self offering you a chance to grow. It is not an ominous shadow, but a spotlight highlighting what you need to learn. Trust that your fears are here to teach you. Facing them is a spiritual practice. Each time you face a fear, you move closer to authenticity. When you step away from fear, you move toward your freedom. Go ahead. Face your fears and forge the path that has always been waiting for you.

What do you fear?

*"Give your Highest Self safe passage to work in your life."*

## Soul R$_x$ #103

## Be Open

After you download a new app, there is often a question asking if the app can access other items on your smartphone like your location or photos. You have two choices: allow or deny access. Being open to life is similar. You can either allow access to life or deny access to life. When you choose openness, you are allowing your Highest Self to work through you. You are giving it safe passage to work in your life.

Being open means:

- **there is an expectation that more goodness is coming your way.** Even if you do not get everything you want, you realize you got more than you expected or your openness lead you to a new opportunity.

- **recognizing what is possible.** Just because you cannot see something yet, does not mean it is not possible.

- **being gentle with yourself.** Allow yourself to dream. Be light. Do not always take yourself so seriously. Refrain from beating yourself up. Sometimes the only schoolyard bully is the one that exists within you.

- **having an open heart.** Take down the walls. Allow love in instead of rejecting it. Accept compliments, smile at people, make connections. Be a multiplier of love, not a divider. The world needs it.

Being closed feels safe and protected, but it also feels immobilizing and unexciting. Closing yourself off is a defense mechanism to avoid rejection, hurt, or disappointment, but in doing so you are also denying access to creativity, inspiration, love, compassion, possibility, and personal power. There is so much good waiting for you that far outweighs the bad. Do not live jaded and guarded about life. Make the connection with your Highest Self stronger than the one with your Ego. Goodness will follow the path of least resistance. Make it easy for goodness to reach you.

How would being more open serve you?

*"Detachment is freedom."*

## Soul R<sub>x</sub> #104

## *Detach Yourself From The Outcome*

Think of a situation where you wished for a certain outcome. How much did you obsess over it hoping you could influence it? Most likely the situation was out of your control. Think of the angst, worry, and pain that ensued as a result of your obsession. When you spend time in angst, worry and self-inflicted pain, you willingly walk away from your Highest Self where your joy resides. You purposefully choose pain over joy. Detaching yourself from an outcome is a form of letting go. Let go of trying to control the ending. The more closely you are held to the outcome, the more suffering you endure. Detachment is freedom.

When you value your relationship with your Highest Self and are not willing to give up your joy, you will seek ways to maintain that connection. Detaching yourself from the outcome is a way to maintain your joyful status.

Detaching yourself from the outcome says:

- I am going to worry less.
- I want peace more than I want suffering.
- I do not need the outcome that I envision in order to be happy.
- My way is not the only way.
- I am open to change.
- I am open to new ideas.
- I am willing to be flexible.
- I am not willing to disturb someone else's peace.

Detachment is spiritual maturity.

What would detaching yourself from outcomes give you?

## Acknowledgements

Getting this book written was a long time dream. Dreams take work to bring to fruition and dreams need a team to get them accomplished. I want to thank Joanne MacMillan, my long time friend and now editor and encourager extraordinaire. Your willingness to walk this writing road with me gave me motivation to start and finish my dream. On days when I struggled with writing or questioned myself, you gently encouraged me to continue. You refocused my attention so that I could get back to writing. I am grateful for your friendship, feedback and your commitment to getting me published.

Thanks to my friend, Elaine Shannon, who in combination with Joanne MacMillan and myself, banded together to start a small writing group. Your laughter and encouragement made the journey fun. Our regular writing meetings validated my writing journey. It was within this group that I learned to share fearlessly. The ability to laugh at ourselves and share without judgement kept the walls from going up so that writing became an imperfect act. It is through the unknowing encouragement to write imperfectly that this book was able to be birthed.

Thanks to, Barb Stillman and Mike Blanchet who were the first readers of *Soul Prescription 101 Ways to find Joy, Meaning & Fulfillment*. Your feedback was so valuable allowing me to breathe a sigh of relief. I greatly appreciate your willingness to give your time and thoughts to my writing. Thank you for your testimonials too.

Thank you to Skye Dyer for reading my book and for providing your reflections for the Foreword. I am grateful for your contribution.

Thank you to Paul Martinelli for allowing me to share your story.

To my husband, Eric, who is my best friend and spiritual partner. Thank you for your support. You have talked me off ledges. You have talked me onto ledges. You have encouraged me to leap never once discouraging me from my dreams. I love you and thank you for always believing in me. You saw me before I saw me.

To my children, Lucas and Julia, I love your creativity and your curiosity. As your mother, I was always ready to be your teacher, but so often I have found that I have been the student. I have learned so much from you. Thank you for being interested in my dreams and for thinking that what I was trying to achieve was "cool." I love you.

To my parents, Larry and Rose, thank you for being storytellers and for being great examples of work ethic and excellence. Thank you for your sense of humor. My ability to not take myself so seriously helped me write this book. I love you both.

To all those who knew I was writing a book, your encouraging comments and expressed desire to read it were oxygen to the writing process.

To those who liked, commented and shared my daily social media posts in the year leading up to the launch of this book, I thank you. To begin sharing your thoughts publicly is to step out and be seen. That is scary. My desire was to encourage you, but through your support, you encouraged me.

To my graphic designer friend, Sonya MacAskill of Crystal Clear Designs. Thank you for designing the exterior of my book. It is a beautiful design. You are a talent and you gave me more than I asked.

To Mark Pridham, thank you for the beautiful author photo located on the back of my book. You captured my spirit. (The Pridham Group, www.thepridhamgroup.com).

Blessings to you all.

# About The Author

Dana Lloyd is a Leadership Coach and Keynote Speaker who lives in Rothesay, New Brunswick. Dana speaks, trains and coaches on leading well, personally and professionally.

Dana received her Bachelor of Education at the University of New Brunswick. After University, Dana began her career in the corporate world. During that time, questions began to rise about what she should be doing with her life. She shares her struggle with discontentment and how she found her own path.

Naturally introspective, Dana is determined to consistently lead a joy filled life. Her purpose is to inspire and empower people to live fulfilled lives. This book is a compilation of lessons as well as practical ways to find joy, meaning and fulfillment. It is Dana's wish that others will see their lives in a new light allowing them to step into their greatness knowing they already have the power to create the life they want.

You can connect with Dana Lloyd at www.DanaLloydLeadership.com

www.ingramcontent.com/pod-product-compliance
Lightning Source LLC
Chambersburg PA
CBHW032104090426
42743CB00007B/226